J. A. G. GRIFFITH was born in 1918 and educated at Taunton School and the London School of Economics and Political Science (LSE). He has been on the staff of LSE since 1948, becoming Professor of English Law in 1959 and of Public Law in 1970. Since 1956 he has edited *Public Law*. His books include *Principles of Administrative Law* (with H. Street), *Central Departments and Local Authorities*, *Government and Law* (with T. C. Hartley), and *Parliamentary Scrutiny of Government Bills*. He is honorary secretary of the Council for Academic Freedom and Democracy and a regular contributor to the *New Statesman*.

Political Issues of Modern Britain
Editors: Bernard Crick and Patrick Seyd

PUBLISHED
The Politics of the Media John Whale

FORTHCOMING
The Politics of Educational Change Maurice Kogan
The Politics of Race Relations Dipak Nandy
The Politics of Industrial Relations Colin Crouch
The Politics of Economic Planning Alan Budd

The
Politics of the Judiciary

J. A. G. GRIFFITH

Fontana/Collins

Published by Fontana in 1977
Second Impression April 1978
Third Impression March 1979

The Politics of the Judiciary is published
in hardback by Manchester University Press

Copyright © J. A. G. Griffith 1977

Made and printed in Great Britain by
William Collins Sons & Co Ltd, Glasgow

To
BEN
who helped

Juger l'administration, c'est aussi administrer
                    J.–E.–M. Portalis 1745-1807

*The vanity of appearing as model employers of Labour
had not then, apparently, taken possession of the
council, nor had the council become such ardent
feminists as to bring about, at the expense of the
ratepayers whose money they administered, sex
equality in the labour market . . . The council would,
in my view, fail in their duty if, in administering funds
which did not belong to their members alone, they
put aside all these aims to the ascertainment of what
was just and reasonable remuneration to give for the
services rendered to them, and allowed themselves
to be guided in preference by some eccentric
principles of socialistic philanthropy, or by a feminist
ambition to secure the equality of the sexes in the
matter of wages in the world of labour.*

                    Lord Atkinson in
                    Roberts v. Hopwood [1925] A.C. 578.

Contents

Contents

Editors' preface

This new series aims to put into the hands of the intelligent general reader concise and authoritative accounts of the major issues of British politics today. Writing on politics has too often suffered from being either strident polemic or ephemeral journalism or else from being academic monographs too specialized and technical for the general reader. This series hopes to fill this important gap in what has been called 'the dead ground of contemporary history' (that is, it is more difficult to find reliable accounts of what happened ten or twenty years ago than fifty) by covering the issues which opinion polls and specialized opinion have judged to be the major issues of contemporary British politics. We say 'issues' deliberately and not *problems*. Perhaps, indeed, beneath all these political issues there are fundamental economic and social problems. Theories are not lacking to explain them all and to put them all in a 'correct theoretical perspective'. Our aim is more modest and precise: to remedy the lack of books that give accounts of the issues which, doubtless, reflect forces more fundamental.

Each book will cover three main topics and, ordinarily, will be in this form: (i) a brief summary of the origins of the issue and fuller account of its history since the Second World War; (ii) an account of its institutional setting and of the pressure groups associated with the issues; and (iii) an account of what should be done and what is likely to happen. We ask each author to be as objective and as balanced as is possible in the first two sections, but as polemical and as stimulating as he or she cares to or thinks fit in the third.

The series aims to achieve the same high standards of judgment but also of brevity that have been typical of the

Fontana *MODERN MASTERS* series, that is to be intellectually demanding but completely non-technical. It aims to fulfil much the same function: both to be an intelligent and readily comprehensible introduction to the general reader and to be a way in which a specialist in one field can communicate with a specialist in another. If we may draw an analogy, we have briefed our authors to attempt that intellectually demanding but completely non-technical level of writing that is typical of the *Political Quarterly* at its best. Yet while the series is primarily intended for the educated general reader, students of history, politics, economics and social administration will find that the books fill a gap. They reflect a growing concern in the academic study of politics to look first at actual issues, rather than at institutions or methodologies.

If new editions are warranted, the first and second sections of each book will, of course, be revised. But each time there is a reprint, we will ask the author to update the third section on policy, on what is being done. Thus each reprint will be topical while the edition places the issue in a deeper historical and institutional setting. We hope that this novel feature of the series will help it to be a contribution to what Walter Bagehot once called 'the political education of mankind'. For that education seems at the moment so often to suffer from books which are a strange mixture of abstract theory and instant polemic. Issues need studying in an historical context if we are to act sensibly and effectively; but act we must.

BERNARD CRICK
PATRICK SEYD

Preface

When I had written the first draft of this book, I sent it for destructive criticism to these friends of mine: David Bentley, Bernard Crick, Joe Jacob, Ralph Miliband, John Saville, Bill Wedderburn and John Westergaard. They obliged, as true friends will, and I am greatly in their debt. But since this is, I hope, a controversial book, and since the final draft (which none of them saw) differs in many important particulars from what they read, it is for once important to emphasize that only I am responsible for the views here expressed.

Apart from those named, many colleagues and others responded to my enquiries or gave me their views and I am grateful to them also. Once again, I thank the staff of the British Library of Political and Economic Science who, as always, were as helpful as they could possibly have been.

In the preface to my last book I said that 'not for the first nor (I hope) for the last time' I was greatly indebted to Miss Colleen Etheridge who bears with remarkable fortitude the burden of being my secretary. I repeat that hope and those sincere thanks.

JOHN GRIFFITH

London School of Economics
& Political Science
Houghton Street
London, W.C.2

PART ONE

The Judiciary

> There is one matter which I ought to mention. All the judges, without exception, are members of the Athenaeum, and I presume you will wish to be a member. If so, may I have the pleasure of proposing you? There is a meeting of the Committee early next week.

Lord Cozens-Hardy, MR to Lord Buckmaster—as he became—on the latter's appointment to the Lord Chancellorship, in a letter dated 26 May 1915, quoted by R. F. V. Heuston, *The Lives of the Lord Chancellors 1885-1940*, page 269.

Chapter 1: Courts and judges

INTRODUCTION

This book is concerned with the relationship between the judiciary and politics. In the courts political questions may come before the judges because the matter is already in public controversy, like race or industrial relations; or because the matter concerns some form of protest or demonstration against established authority, as with students or minority groups; or because the matter concerns the exercise of powers by the police; or because the matter impinges on the individual rights of citizens, affecting their freedom or their property.

The laws relating to civil and criminal wrongs are made either by Parliament in the form of Acts of Parliament (also called statutes) or by the judges themselves (called the common law). The common law is made as judges decide cases and state the principles on which they are basing their decisions, this accumulation of principles building into a body of law. Some parts of this common law have long fallen into disuse as having no contemporary relevance. Other parts have evolved to meet social changes. Statute law, however, predominates over common law wherever there is conflict and much statute law is made to change and to replace parts of the common law.

Statute law itself cannot be a perfect instrument. A statute or one section of a statute may be made to deal with some particular subject – perhaps with immigration, or drugs, or housing or education – but a situation arises where doubt is cast on the meaning of the words of the statute. Does the situation fall within these words or not? For example, do the words 'national origins' include 'nationality'? (see below, pp. 87-8) The judges then must decide how to interpret the statute and by so doing they define its meaning. Not only therefore do the judges 'make law' through the development of the common law. They also do so by this process of statutory interpretation.

Judges are employed to decide disputes. Sometimes these disputes are between private individuals as when neighbours disagree or one person is injured by another in an accident. Sometimes these disputes may be between large private organizations as when companies argue about the terms of a commercial contract. But public bodies – Government departments, local authorities, nationalized industries and others – are also legal persons and also become involved in disputes which lead to judicial activity. The fact that one of the parties is a public body does not necessarily affect the nature of the dispute or the law applicable to it. If a Government department or the Greater London Council or the Post Office enters into a contract with a building company for the construction of a block of offices, and a dispute arises, the law which governs the matter is essentially the same as it would be if the contract were between two private persons.

Such disputes are dealt with by the civil law and in the civil courts. The judgment given will say where the rights and wrongs lie and the court may award damages to one party or even order a party to take certain positive steps or to refrain from certain action.

In criminal law, the dispute is with the State. Over the years laws have been made and amended declaring certain kinds of action to be criminal and punishable with imprisonment or fines. This has been done because it is believed that the State has an interest in seeking to prevent those actions and to punish those who so act. So we have crimes called murder, manslaughter, rape, conspiracy, theft, fraud, assault, and hundreds of others, some of them quite trivial. They are dealt with in the criminal courts.[1]

If the judicial function were wholly automatic, then not only would the making of decisions in the courts be of little interest but it would also not be necessary to recruit highly trained and intellectually able men and women to serve as judges and to pay them handsome salaries.

It is the creative function of judges (see further, below, chapter 8) that makes their job important and makes worthwhile some assessment of the way they behave, especially in political cases. It must be remembered that in most cases for most of the time the function of the judge (with the help of the jury if there is one) is to ascertain the facts. But when questions of law do arise, their determination may be of the greatest importance because of the effect that will have on subsequent cases.

APPOINTMENT

The most remarkable fact about the appointment of judges is that it is wholly in the hands of politicians.[2] High Court and Circuit judges, Recorders, stipendiary and lay magistrates are appointed by or on the advice of the Lord Chancellor who is a member of the Cabinet. Appointments to the Court of Appeal, to the Judicial Committee of the House of Lords[3], and to the offices of Lord Chief Justice and President of the Family Division are made on the advice of the Prime Minister after consultation with the Lord Chancellor, who himself consults with senior members of the judiciary before making his choice or consulting with the Prime Minister. The Lord Chancellor has his own Department headed, since the 1880s, by a permanent secretary. The Department is the centre for the collection of information about the activity, the legal practice, and the reputation of members of the bar including those more senior, almost always Queen's Counsel (the conferment of which status is in the gift of the Lord Chancellor), from whom senior judicial appointments will be made. Inevitably the officials in the Department exercise some influence but the extent of this varies and is difficult to assess.

How far the Prime Minister uses his power of appointment or, to put this another way, how far he merely accepts the Lord Chancellor's advice on senior appointments varies with different Prime Ministers and differing circumstances. It seems to be unusual for the Prime Minister or the Lord Chancellor to consult other Ministers (except that the Lord Chancellor may discuss the matter with the Attorney-General and the Solicitor-General) unless any such Minister happens to be also a distinguished member of the bar, as was Sir Stafford Cripps in Mr Attlee's administration from 1945. But it would be a mistake to assume that Prime Ministers are necessarily mouth-pieces of their Lord Chancellors when making these appointments.

Lord Simon of Glaisdale has written:[4] 'In 1951 Sir Winston [Churchill] particularly wanted [Sir Walter Monckton] in the unenviable post of Minister of Labour, and (presumably by way of compensation) undertook in writing that he should be appointed Lord Chief Justice on the next vacancy.'

Such an undertaking must have been of very little value. Lord Goddard was then in only his sixth year as Lord Chief Justice, never looked like someone about to retire, and indeed continued in office for three years after Sir Winston gave way as Prime Minister in 1955. But the story shows that Sir Winston had no doubt that the office was solely in his gift.

Although Prime Ministers may from time to time use words which suggest that they are not unwilling to exercise their power of appointment, in recent times there is no evidence that they have done so. The likelihood is that a modern Prime Minister would depart from the recommendations of his Lord Chancellor only in the most exceptional case.

Solicitors and barristers may be appointed as Recorders or stipendiary magistrates. A Recorder who has served for five years may be appointed as a Circuit judge. Otherwise judges are appointed from the ranks of barristers of at least ten or fifteen years standing and are likely to have had at least twenty years' practice at the bar. Judges in the Court of Appeal are usually appointed from amongst High Court judges and Law Lords from amongst Appeal Court judges.[5]

In 1976 the Lord Chancellor was paid £17,500 per annum as a judge[6], Lords of Appeal in Ordinary (Law Lords) and the Master of the Rolls were paid £21,175; Lords Justices of Appeal (in the Court of Appeal) £19,425; the President of the Family Division was paid £20,175 and the Lord Chief Justice £19,100; judges of the High Court were paid £18,675; Circuit judges £13,000.

From these figures it will be seen that High Court judges gain little financially from promotion. And at present Circuit judges are not often promoted to the High Court. Judges of the High Court and above, with the exception of the Lord Chancellor, hold office during good behaviour subject to a power of removal by Her Majesty on an address presented by both Houses of Parliament but no English judge has been removed under this provision which derives from the Act of Settlement 1701. Circuit judges, and Recorders, however, may be removed from office by the Lord Chancellor on the ground of incapacity or misbehaviour. Magistrates are removable by the Lord Chancellor for good cause. Senior judges must retire at 75 years of age, Circuit judges at 72 with possible extension to 75, justices of the peace and stipendiaries at 70.

Judges of the superior courts may not be sued for anything done or said while acting in their judicial capacity even if they act from some malicious or corrupt motive. The law does permit judges to be prosecuted for crimes they may commit but proof of criminal intent would be extremely difficult even if an appropriate charge could be devised.[7]

To what extent, if at all, do the Lord Chancellor and the Prime Minister take into account the political allegiance of those whom they appoint or promote to judicial office?

First, there is one special case. The Attorney-General and the Solicitor-General (the law officers of the Crown) are Ministers, not in the Cabinet, appointed by the Prime Minister from the ranks of Members of the House of Commons who are barristers. It is often said that by

19

tradition they have a right to judicial appointment when vacancies occur and that this is particularly true of appointment to the office of Lord Chief Justice. In a famous essay, H. J. Laski recorded that between 1832 and 1906, out of 139 judges appointed, 80 were Members of the House of Commons at the time of their nomination and 11 others had been candidates for Parliament; that, of the 80, 63 were appointed by their own party while in office; and 33 of them had been either Attorney-General or Solicitor-General.[8] Laski suggested that it was 'probably undesirable' for law officers to be suddenly made judges and so required to act impartially. Laski treads very daintily here. 'It is not necessary to suggest that there will be conscious unfairness; but it is, I submit, possible that such judges will, particularly in cases where the liberty of the subject is concerned, find themselves unconsciously biased through over-appreciation of executive difficulty ... Nothing is more disastrous than that any suspicion of the complete impartiality of the judges should be possible.'

In 1937 a Member of Parliament said in the House of Commons that every Government took it for granted that the law officers had the right to 'certain high positions in the State regardless whether they happen to be the most suitable persons' and he instanced the offices of Master of the Rolls and Lord Chancellor. But a Government spokesman denied this saying that the law officers had never put forward such a proposition and that there was 'no foundation' for it.[9]

The tradition is certainly weaker today but by no means dead. In 1962, the Solicitor-General was appointed to the Presidency of what was then the Probate, Divorce and Admiralty Division of the High Court. And Attorneys-General, then or previously in that office, may be strong candidates for appointment as Lord Chancellor though the political nature of that office distinguishes it from appointments to purely judicial office. It is perhaps significant that none of the last three Lord Chief Justices – Lords Goddard, Parker and Widgery – had been law officers. It may be that, today, law officers have greater expectations of political promotion and prefer to pursue that ambition. Nevertheless if they wished to become judges and vacancies occurred appropriately, it must be supposed they would always be strong candidates.

The wider question, also raised by Laski's figures, is the extent to which an active political life, and particularly Membership of the House of Commons, is regarded by the Lord Chancellor as a positive qualification for appointment to a judgeship. Practice has differed over the years.

Lord Halsbury was Lord Chancellor for far longer than any other during the last 100 years. He had three periods in that office which he held, in all, for over seventeen years between 1885 and 1905. His judicial appointments were much criticized on the ground in effect that 'Halsbury appointed to the High Court, and to a lesser extent to the county court, men of little or no legal learning whose previous career in public life had been largely in the service of the Conservative Party or else were relations of his own'.[10] Professor Heuston has examined such criticisms. Of the thirty judges appointed by Halsbury to the High Court, eight were MPs at the date of their appointment and of these six were Conservatives. Five others had been unsuccessful Parliamentary candidates, three of them being Conservatives. One other had been a Conservative MP nearly twenty years before. So fourteen out of the thirty appointments were, in those senses, of politicians – and ten were Conservatives. Heuston concludes that of Halsbury's 30 appointments to the High Court, four or five were men of real distinction, eighteen or nineteen were men of competent professional attainments, leaving no more than seven 'whose appointments seem dubious'. Four of these seven were Conservative MPs at the date of their appointment, one had been a Conservative MP, and another had twice been an unsuccessful Conservative candidate. We may say, therefore (this is my conclusion not Heuston's), that of the ten Conservative politicians whom Halsbury appointed, six were bad appointments. Every Lord Chancellor, especially if he holds office as long as did Halsbury, will make some mistakes (and Heuston suggests that as many as three of the six were 'unlucky' appointments) but Halsbury's experience may suggest that the proportion of bad appointments is likely to be statistically higher amongst appointments made from the Lord Chancellor's political associates.

Certainly at that time it was accepted that a political career was likely to be an advantage for a barrister aspiring to a judgeship, though it was important that his seat should be safe, as no Government would wish to run the possibility of diminishing its strength in the House. Heuston tells us how Lord Halsbury when he was a Parliamentary candidate was congratulated by Sir Edward Clarke on his election defeat by nine votes in 1874. Clarke explained that if Halsbury had won by such a majority he could not have expected elevation to a judgeship. But, as it was, he could expect to be made Solicitor-General and found a safe seat. This is indeed what happened although he held the office for over a year until the seat was found for him in 1877. (During the interval he was in fact offered a judgeship, which he declined, but it was made clear that the Government could not long countenance a Solicitor-General without a seat in the House of Commons.)

In August 1895, arising out of argument about the fees payable to the law officers, Lord Salisbury, as Prime Minister, promised Sir Edward Clarke that he would be appointed Attorney-General if a vacancy occurred within two years. In 1897, a new Master of the Rolls had to be appointed. If the Attorney-General (Sir Richard Webster) took the post, Clarke would have to be appointed Attorney-General. Lord Salisbury, who had a poor opinion of Clarke's abilities (as had Halsbury) wrote in much perplexity to the Lord Chancellor but saying that the Rolls should be offered to Clarke 'on party grounds' because he would do less harm as a judge than as Attorney-General. Salisbury continued:

There remains the third course, to throw Clarke over altogether and tell him that the highest point of his career has been reached. I confess that the more I consider this alternative, the more I dislike it. It is at variance with the unwritten law of our party system; and there is no clearer statute in that unwritten law than the rule that party claims should always weigh very heavily in the disposal of the highest legal appointments . . . It would be a breach of the tacit convention on which politicians and lawyers have worked the British Constitution together for the last 200 years. Perhaps it is not an ideal system – some day no doubt the MR will be appointed by competitive examination in Law Reports, but it is our system for the present; and we should give our party arrangements a wrench if we throw it aside.

Lord Salisbury did offer the Rolls to Clarke who declined it on the ground that it would put an end to his political career, though he added that he would accept being a Law Lord. But that offer did not come.[11]

The change in the attitude to the appointment of barrister-politicians as judges is said to date from Lord Haldane's Chancellorship (1912-15) when legal and professional qualifications became the criteria, though at first the change was not extended to the most senior appointments. Lord Haldane himself expressed his 'strong conviction that, at all events for a judge who is to sit in the Supreme Tribunals of the Empire, a House of Commons training is a real advantage. One learns there the nuances of the Constitution, and phases of individual and social political life which are invaluable in checking the danger of abstractedness in mental outlook.'[12]

But a little later Lord Sankey, who was Lord Chancellor from 1929 to 1935, when resignations occurred, replaced five Law Lords who had had political backgrounds by others whose reputations rested on their professionalism as lawyers.[13]

In recent years Lord Chancellors have differed in their opinions about the value of judges having had experience as politicians. During the 1950s, being an MP came once again to be regarded as a qualification for appointment to a judgeship. In 1964, Lord Gardiner, who shortly afterwards became Lord Chancellor himself, said that since 1951 'one or two' Lord Chancellors (there had been only three) 'felt that the standard of members of the bar going into the House of Commons has fallen noticeably since the war, and if you want the right men in the House of Commons then you must reward the man who votes the right way with a judgeship'.[14] Lord Gardiner himself thought that political views ought not to affect judicial appointments at all, and he pursued this policy during his period of office as Lord Chancellor (1964-70).

Today, being an active member of a political party seems to be neither a qualification nor a disqualification for appointment.

It must be remembered that Lord Chancellors in making their appointments to the High Court have a relatively small group to select from. Effectively, the group consists of experienced barristers between the ages of 45 and 60 and the number of genuine possibilities – the short list – may be as small as half a dozen.

Personal characteristics must be taken into account. A man or woman whose social or personal habits are unconventional or uncertain is not likely to be risked. On the other hand, it is obvious from the appointments made that the strength of a candidate's convictions, including his political opinions, is not considered a disadvantage. But those opinions should fall within the ordinary range represented in the House of Commons.

SOCIAL AND POLITICAL POSITION

From time to time in recent years, analyses have been made, based on information in reference books, of the social background of the more senior judiciary.

24

The most comprehensive in terms simply of social class origins[15] covers the period from 1820-1968.

Period of Appointment	1820-1875	1876-1920	1921-1950	1951-1968	1820-1968	Number
Social class I Traditional landed upper class	% 17·9	% 16·4	% 15·4	% 10·5	% 15·3	59
II Professional, commercial and administrative upper class	8·5	14·6	14·3	14·0	12·7	49
III Upper middle class	40·6	50·5	47·3	52·3	47·4	183
IV Lower middle class	11·3	9·7	8·8	8·1	9·6	37
V Working class	2·8	1·0	1·1	1·2	1·3	6
Not known	18·9	7·8	13·2	14·0	13·5	52
	100	100	100	100	100	
Number	106	103	91	86	386	386

Over the whole period the dominance of the upper and upper middle classes is overwhelming. They account for 75.4 per cent to which may be added, proportionately, 10 per cent from those 'not known'. Moreover the total percentage of these first three groups in the most recent period is 76.8, which is higher than the overall percentage. Over the whole period covered by this analysis the dominance of the first three classes is unchanged.[16]

Another survey, published in 1975, covers the period 1876-1972 and, with a few omissions, analyses the 317 judges who sat in the High Court, the Court of Appeal and the House of Lords during that period. The author does not, however, break down these 96 years into shorter periods so trends within the whole are not apparent. He considers school background and finds that 33 per cent attended one of the nine most famous public schools[17] while 70 per cent attended Oxford or Cambridge Universities.[18]

School education is a good indicator of social and economic class background, particularly as the relative cost of attendance at one of the independent 'public' schools has changed little, until very recently. It must also be remembered that university education at Oxford and Cambridge before 1945 (when those who are now judges attended) was also very largely a middle-class activity, within the first three groups of the table set out above.

In 1956 the *Economist*[19] published a short survey. This covered 69 judges of the Supreme Court, House of Lords and Judicial Committee of the Privy Council and showed that 76 per cent had attended 'major public schools' (not further defined) and the same percentage had been to Oxford or Cambridge. In May 1970 *New Society*[20] looked at 359 judges including those offices surveyed by the *Economist* but also, amongst others, county court judgeships and metropolitan magistrates. This found that 81 per cent had attended public schools and 76 per cent had attended Oxford or Cambridge. In 1969, Henry Cecil investigated the background of 117 out of 235 judges of the House of Lords, the Supreme Court, county courts and stipendiary magistrates. From a random group of 36 judges of the Court of Appeal and the High Court, he found that 31 had been to public schools (86 per cent) and 33 to Oxford or Cambridge (92 per cent). From a random group of 45 (out of 90) county court judges and 24 (out of 48) stipendiaries, he found that 52 had attended public schools (75 per cent) and 56 Oxford or Cambridge (81 per cent). In 1975 Hugo Young analysed the educational background of 31 appointees to the High Court during the previous five years. He found that 68 per cent went to public schools and 74 per cent to Oxford or Cambridge.[21]

These figures have changed very little over the last thirty or more years. In 1940 about 80 per cent of the judges of the Supreme Court had attended public schools. In 1969, this was true of 79 per cent of Henry Cecil's group of 117. A higher proportion of the earlier generation did not attend university at all – eight out of 35 in 1940 but only eight out of 135 in 1970. Of those who did attend, the bias in favour of Oxford and Cambridge has remained effectively unchanged.[22] The *New Society* survey compared county court judges in three recent years. In 1947, in 1957 and in 1967, seven county court judges were appointed. Of these 21 judges, all but one in 1947, two in 1957 and one in 1967 had attended public schools; all but three in 1947, two in 1957 and three in 1967 had attended Oxford or Cambridge.

The decline in the number of 'political' judges is also shown. The *Economist*'s survey of 1956 recorded that 23 per cent of their 69 judges had been MPs or Parliamentary candidates. But fourteen years later, Henry Cecil could find only 10 MPs and 5 candidates out of his 117 judges (13 per cent).

The age of the full-time judiciary has remained constant over many years: the average on appointment has been about 52 or 53 and the average age of all those in office has been about 60. Inevitably, given the system of promotion, the average age is highest in the Court of Appeal and the House of Lords, at about 65 and 68 years respectively.

Since 1876 there have been 63 Lords of Appeal in Ordinary (Law Lords). An analysis of 49 of these showed that 18 had fathers who were lawyers, 16 had fathers of other professions (churchmen, doctors, teachers, architects, soldiers). Twelve fathers were in business (of whom one was working-class), and three fathers were farmers or landowners. Forty-six Law Lords had been to Oxford or

Cambridge, seven to Scottish universities, four to Trinity College Dublin, two to London University (one of whom had also been to Cambridge) and one to Queen's Belfast. These facts and figures added relatively little to what was already known in outline. More interesting is the analysis of political background. The authors[23] divided their period into three groups. Group A included 20 Law Lords appointed in the period 1876-1914; Group B had 21 appointed between 1918 and 1948; Group C had 22 appointed in 1948-69. Of the 20 Law Lords in group A, eleven had been MPs and three Parliamentary candidates; of the 21 in group B, five had been MPs; of the 22 in group C, four had been MPs and two Parliamentary candidates. While these figures show the decline since the late nineteenth and early twentieth century of appointments of such politicians, they also show little change since 1918. It is, however, unwise to base generalizations on such figures. What matters more than prior political involvement is how far Law Lords consciously or otherwise are influenced in their judgments by their own political opinions, how far this is avoidable and how far it is undesirable. One highly 'political' Lord Chancellor – like Lord Hailsham of St Marylebone – can, if he chooses, make a considerable impact on judicial law-making at the highest level but, for this to be so, it is not necessary that he should have held political office or have been a Member of Parliament or a law officer.

All these figures show that, in broad terms, four out of five full-time professional judges are products of public schools, and of Oxford or Cambridge. Very occasionally the brilliant lower-middle-class boy has won his place in this distinguished gathering. With very few exceptions, judges are required to be selected from amongst practising barristers and until recently no one without a private income could survive the first years of practice. To become a successful barrister therefore it was necessary to have financial support and so the background had to be that of the reasonably well-to-do family which, as a matter of course, sent its sons to public schools and then either straight to the bar or first to Oxford or Cambridge. In the last three years, the need for a private income during the first years has to an increasing extent returned.

Nevertheless, some men and women have, since the middle 1960s, benefited from the expansion of university education, from the growth of law faculties in universities, and from the wider availability of this education and, with little private income, have been able (largely because of the increase in publicly financed legal aid) to make a living at the bar. By the mid-1980s some of these will move into the ranks of successful barristers from whom judicial appointments are made. Only then shall we be able to assess how far the dominance of the public schools and (what is of much less significance) of Oxford and Cambridge has begun to lessen. And not until the 1990s shall we know whether (as seems most unlikely) judicial attitudes have changed as a result.

Not yet however can the view of Lord Justice Lawton be accepted. Delivering the Riddell Lecture in 1975 he said that it was a common misconception that the judiciary were drawn from the moneyed classes and educated at leading public schools and at Oxford or Cambridge. In his view judges were 'drawn from all ranks of society' and were 'a microcosm of Britain today'. The learned Lord Justice did not support this view with any evidence.[24]

Judicial independence means that judges are not dependent on Governments in any ways which might influence them in coming to decisions in individual cases. Formally, this independence is preserved by their not being dismissible by the Government of the day. This does not affect their promotion, which, like their appointment, is effectively in the hands of the Lord Chancellor with, nowadays, little or no Prime Ministerial intervention. In financial terms, such promotion is not of much significance. But life in the Court of Appeal and, even more, in the House of Lords is not so strenuous as in the High Court (or below), personal prestige and status are higher among the fewer, with a life peerage at the top. These are not inconsiderable rewards for promotion, and the question is whether there are pressures on, particularly, High Court judges to act and to speak in court in certain ways rather than in others. Are there decisions which could be classified as popular or unpopular in the eyes of the most important senior judges or the Lord Chancellor? Is a judge ever conscious that his reputation as a judge is likely to be adversely affected in their eyes if he decides one way, and favourably affected if he decides another way?

The answer is that such pressures do exist. For example, a judge who acquires a reputation among his seniors for being 'soft' in certain types of cases where the Lord Chancellor, the Lord Chief Justice, the Master of the Rolls and other senior judges favour a hard line is likely to damage his promotion prospects as he would if his appointment were found to be unfortunate on other more obvious grounds. But this does not amount to dependence on the political wishes of Governments or Ministers as such. In no real sense does such direct dependence or influence exist. How far judges consciously or unconsciously subserve the wider interests of Governments is another and more important question.

What is meant by saying that judges must be impartial and seen to be so? Judges themselves claim this as their great virtue and only occasionally is it seen to be departed from. Lord Haldane was a practising barrister in 1901 when he recorded:

I fought my hardest for the Dutch prisoners before the Privy Council this morning, but the tribunal was hopelessly divided, and the anti-Boers prevailed over the pro-Boers. It is bad that so much bias should be shewn, but it is, I suppose, inevitable.[25]

D. N. Pritt in his autobiography told of his many political cases and of one which 'came before a judge of great experience and knowledge, so bitterly opposed to anything left-wing that he could scarcely have given a fair trial if he had tried'.[26]

Are such phrases applicable today? Every practising barrister knows before which judges he would prefer not to appear in a political case because he believes, and his colleagues at the bar believe, that certain judges are much more likely than others to be biased against certain groups, like demonstrators or students, or certain kinds of action, like occupations of property by trade unionists or the homeless.

This however is to say little more than that, as we have already remarked, judges are human with human prejudices. And that some are more human than others. But if that were all we would expect to find a wide spectrum of judicial opinion about political cases. Instead, we find a remarkable consistency of approach in these cases concentrated in a fairly narrow part of the spectrum of political opinion. It spreads from that part of the centre which is shared by right-wing Labour, Liberal and 'progressive' Conservative opinion to that part of the right which is associated with traditional Toryism – but not beyond into the reaches of the far right.

A NOTE ON THE STRUCTURE OF COURTS

Civil cases are first heard either in county courts by Circuit judges (of whom there are some 260); or in the High Court by judges of the High Court[27] (of whom there are about 70). Each case is heard by a single judge (very occasionally with a jury).[28] The High Court is divided into the Queen's Bench, Chancery, and Family Divisions. The head of the Queen's Bench is the Lord Chief Justice, of the Chancery is the Vice-Chancellor, and of the Family Division is its President. For certain cases two or three judges of the Queen's Bench sit together (normally the Lord Chief Justice is one of them) and are then called the Divisional Court of the Queen's Bench Division.[29]

CIVIL JURISDICTION

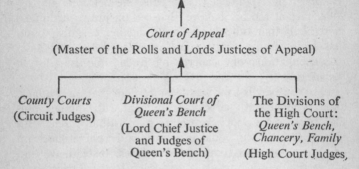

House of Lords (Judicial Committee)
(Lords of Appeal in Ordinary also called Law Lords)

↑

Court of Appeal
(Master of the Rolls and Lords Justices of Appeal)

↑

| *County Courts*
(Circuit Judges) | *Divisional Court of*
Queen's Bench
(Lord Chief Justice
and Judges of
Queen's Bench) | The Divisions of
the High Court:
Queen's Bench,
Chancery, Family
(High Court Judges) |

Appeal from county courts and the High Court lies to the Court of Appeal (civil division) which is presided over by the Master of the Rolls and where the other judges are called Lords Justices of Appeal (of whom there are fourteen). Three judges usually sit on each case. From the Court of Appeal, appeal may lie to the House of Lords in important cases. The House of Lords for this purpose consists of the Lord Chancellor (who sits infrequently) and the Lords of Appeal in Ordinary (Law Lords, of whom there are not more than eleven). Other peers who hold or have held high judicial office (normally about 12 in number) may sit but rarely do so. Five usually sit on each case. For an appeal to the House of Lords, either the Court of Appeal or the House of Lords must give leave. It is possible, in certain circumstances, again if leave is obtained, to appeal direct from the High Court to the House of Lords, leapfrogging the Court of Appeal.

Less serious *criminal* cases are tried summarily (without a jury) by magistrates' courts where sit either two or more lay Justices of the Peace (of whom there are some 18,000) or a legally-qualified stipendiary magistrate (of whom there

CRIMINAL JURISDICTION

House of Lords (Judicial Committee)
(Lords of Appeal in Ordinary also called Law Lords)

Divisional Court of Queen's Bench
(Lord Chief Justice and Judges
of Queen's Bench)

Court of Appeal
(Lord Chief Justice,
Lords Justices of Appeal
and High Court Judges)

Crown Court
(Queen's Bench and Circuit
Judges, Recorders, J.P.s)

Magistrates' Courts
(J.P.s, Stipendiaries)

are about 50, mostly sitting in London). More serious
criminal cases are first enquired into by magistrates' courts
to see if there is sufficient evidence for the case to go
further. If there is, the case goes to the Crown Court
(sitting with a jury and in many different places) where it
is heard by a Queen's Bench or Circuit judge or by a
Recorder (in certain circumstances joined by two to four
Justices of the Peace). Recorders (of whom there are some
350) are practising barristers or solicitors who are required
to sit for a few weeks each year.

Appeals from decisions of magistrates' courts on less
serious cases go either, if only a question of law is disputed,
to the Divisional Court of the Queen's Bench Division or,
where the appeal is on questions of fact and/or law, to
the Crown Court. Appeals from decisions in more serious
cases (heard originally by the Crown Court) go to the

Court of Appeal (criminal division) which draws its members from the Lord Chief Justice, the Lords Justices of Appeal and the Judges of the High Court. Normally, three sit on each case. From the Divisional Court and the Court of Appeal, further appeal lies to the House of Lords if leave is obtained.

The Court of Appeal, the High Court and the Crown Court are together known as the Supreme Court of Judicature.

Finally, the Judicial Committee of the Privy Council hears appeals from a very limited number of overseas territories. It is composed of Law Lords, and others who hold or have held high judicial office in the United Kingdom or the Commonwealth.

NOTES

1. The structure of the civil and criminal courts is summarized on pp. 31-4.

2. For a recent general account see S. Shetreet, *Judges on Trial*, 1976.

3. Referred to hereafter simply as the House of Lords.

4. 81 L.Q.R. 295 (1965).

5. The Lord Chancellor need have no legal qualifications whatever, but in practice is appointed from the ranks of those senior barristers who are members of the political party of the government.

6. And £2500 as 'Speaker' of the House of Lords.

7. For recent authority see *Sirros v. Moore* (1975) Q.B. 118 and Margaret Brazier 'Judicial Immunity and the Independence of the Judiciary' in [1976] *Public Law* 397.

8. H. J. Laski, *Studies in Law and Politics*, pp. 164-80.

9. 324 H. C Deb. col. 1202. See J Ll. J. Edwards. *The Law Officers of the Crown*, especially chapter 15.

10. Heuston *op cit*, p. 36.

11. On all this see Heuston *op cit*, pp 52-4, 323-4.

12. Quoted Heuston *op cit*, p. 39.

13. Abel-Smith and Stevens, *Lawyers and the Courts*.

14. *Economist*, 28 March 1964, p. 210.

15. Class assignment is according to father's occupation or rank. For source see note 16. The judges in this table are those

of the High Court, the Court of Appeal and the House of Lords or of their equivalents.

16. From an unpublished M. Phil. dissertation by Jenny Brock quoted in *The Judiciary*, the report of a Justice Sub-Committee (1972).

17. The so-called Clarendon Schools (Charterhouse, Eton, Harrow, Merchant Taylors, Rugby, St Pauls, Shrewsbury, Westminster, Winchester).

18. C. Neal Tate, *Paths to the Bench in Britain*, 28 Western Political Quarterly 108.

19. December 12, 1956, pp. 946-7

20. 14 May 1970 (by Kevin Goldstein-Jackson).

21. *Sunday Times*, 5 October 1975.

22. Henry Cecil, *The English Judge* (2nd ed. 1972). For a survey of judges sitting on 1 January 1970, see Fred L. Morrison, *Courts and the Political Process in England*, c. 3; the findings are very similar to those in the surveys quoted above.

23. L. Blom-Cooper and G. Drewry, *Final Appeal* (1972).

24. See the *Law Society Gazette*, 18 June 1975.

25. Quoted by Heuston *op cit*, p. 195.

26. *From Right to Left*, p. 142.

27. The numbers of judges etc. are taken from the Law List 1976. At any time there may be a few more or less.

28. Also, registrars (who are solicitors) frequently try small cases in county courts.

29. Very occasionally the other Divisions also adopt this device.

Chapter 2: Extrajudicial activity

Judges are frequently called upon by the Government of the day to preside over commissions, committees and administrative tribunals of different kinds. Some of these are concerned with matters deep in political controversy.

ROYAL COMMISSIONS, DEPARTMENTAL COMMITTEES, AND THE LIKE

Royal commissions are appointed by the Crown to enquire into selected matters of concern.[1] Departmental committees are appointed by Ministers for the same purpose. As the Crown acts on the advice of Ministers in this matter, and as they deal with comparable matters, the distinction between the two is not substantial. Royal commissions have more prestige but nothing of real consequence flows from this, and the matters which these bodies investigate vary greatly in importance.

Dr T. J. Cartwright has recorded that 640 such bodies were appointed between 1945 and 1969 and he examined 358. These included 24 royal commissions; and 334 'major' departmental committees which he defined as those dealing with matters of direct concern to the government of Britain and whose reports were published as command papers.

The mean size of the 24 royal commissions was 13 members but when departmental committees are added the mean size falls to 8 members. Of the 24 royal commissions, judges chaired seven. Only academics equalled them in number of royal commission chairs and no one group[2] of persons held half as many chairs of departmental committees.

Judges chaired commissions or committees concerned with, amongst other things, justices of the peace (1946-8), medical partnerships (1948), police conditions of service (1948-9), the industrial health services (1949-50), State immunities (1949-51), taxation of profits and income (1951-5), marriage and divorce (1951-5), dock workers (1955-6), the interception of communications (1957), prison conditions (1957-8), the working of the monetary system (1957-9), legal education for African students (1960), security in the public service (1961), the security service and Mr Profumo (1963), children and young persons in Scotland (1961-4), jury service (1963-5), the port transport industry (1964-5), pay for dock workers (1966), tribunals of enquiry (1966), 'D' notices (1967), the age of majority (1965-7), trade unions and employers' associations (1965-8), Scottish inshore fisheries (1967-70), the constitution (1969-73), one-parent families (1969-74), and the adoption of children (1969-72). Many of these were highly political, some also highly controversial. Since 1969, important departmental committees chaired by judges have included those on the interrogation of terrorists (1971-2), crowd safety (1971-2), legal procedures to deal with terrorists (1972), the working of the Abortion Act (1971-4), the Red Lion Square disorders (1974-5), and standards of conduct in public life (1974-6).

All those related to affairs within the United Kingdom. In addition, judges have frequently been employed on overseas matters. One of the most famous of these in post-war years was the Nyasaland Commission of Enquiry of 1959 led by Mr Justice Devlin who reported in terms of which the Government of the day did not wholly approve. More recently Lord Pearce chaired a Commission on Rhodesian Opinion (in 1972) appointed to ascertain directly from all sections of the population of Rhodesia whether or not certain proposals for the government of that country were acceptable. The number of such judicial appointments for overseas territories is considerable.

Judges are therefore overwhelmingly the persons most frequently chosen to chair royal commissions and departmental committees, totalling 118 out of Dr Cartwright's 358 bodies. Academics come second with 60 chairmen followed by businessmen with 55. The job is time-consuming and unpaid and this no doubt helps to limit the field of choice.

In addition (and excluded from the examples listed above) judges are normally appointed as chairmen of those numerous committees which are concerned with reform of substantive law or legal procedure. Specifically a judge is chairman of the Law Commission which is the permanent body concerned with law reform. Judges are therefore constantly involved in the process of making recommendations for improvement in the law and this includes not only technical legal subjects but also those on the boundaries of law and politics, like conspiracy. The Scottish Law Commission, also chaired by a judge, has become deeply involved in the debate on devolution, submitting memoranda particularly dealing with the distribution of powers between the United Kingdom Parliament and the proposed Scottish Assembly.[3] These memoranda, although generally avoiding comment that might be regarded as politically partisan on the question of the desirability or otherwise of devolution, contain passages which are bluntly, even scathingly, critical of the statements of the means by which the Government hope to achieve their objectives.

One of the Scottish Law Commission's proposals was that if the area of devolution was sufficiently extensive, responsibility for the courts should also be transferred to the Scottish Assembly. A few months earlier Lord Wheatley spoke on behalf of all the High Court judges in Scotland. He accepted that a judge, as a member of a Royal Commission or a departmental Committee of Enquiry, might have to explain publicly the recommendations arrived at. However, he continued:

When the subject enters the political arena and becomes politically controversial, we assume an elective silence on the political issues and confine ourselves, if we intervene at all, to constitutional or legal questions or views on practical matters affecting the law and its administration, where our views may naturally be expected and sought.[4]

He went on to say that the unanimous view of the High Court judges in Scotland was that the Scottish courts should remain the responsibility of the United Kingdom and not become the responsibility of the Scottish Assembly.

It is difficult to see how this disagreement between the Scottish Law Commission and the Scottish High Court judges could be thought of as other than political.

It is of course a matter of debate how far chairmen, whether judges or not, influence their committees, and no consistent answer is possible. But it is the tradition of chairmen in the United Kingdom to be active. For this reason who is appointed is regarded as being as important as the terms of reference. For many important commissions and committees, those terms are announced first and this is followed some time later by the name of the chairman. Many interests will typically have to be consulted before the chairman is decided on and thereafter his views on the membership will be sought. Far more than any other member, the chairman is privy to the Government's hopes and intentions, and contact between him and the Minister or Ministers concerned will often be close and may well be continuous.

Judges also preside over enquiries set up under the Tribunals of Enquiry (Evidence) Act 1921. These enquiries are nowadays reserved for investigations into matters which may involve the reputation of Ministers or public officials. Between 1945 and 1970 there were five: in 1948-9 into questions of possible bribery of Ministers, chaired by Mr Justice Lynskey[5]; in 1957-8 into leakage of bank rate, chaired by Lord Justice Parker[6]; in 1959 into allegations of police assault on a boy, chaired by Lord Sorn[7]; in 1962-3 into a case of spying in which a Minister's moral behaviour might have been involved, chaired by Lord Radcliffe[8]; and in 1966-7 into the responsibility for the Aberfan disaster, chaired by Lord Justice Edmund

Davies[9]. Since 1970, this procedure has been used twice in Northern Ireland, as we shall see.[10] In 1972 a Tribunal of Enquiry presided over by Mr Justice James enquired into the collapse of the Vehicle and General Insurance Company and reported in terms which were critical in particular of one civil servant.[11]

Three outstanding examples of the use of the judiciary in politics are to be found in the control of restrictive practices, industrial relations, and Northern Ireland.

THE RESTRICTIVE PRACTICES COURT

The Restrictive Practices Court was established under an Act of 1956 and consisted of five judges and not more than ten other members qualified by virtue of their knowledge of or experience in industry, commerce or public affairs. The function of the Court is to decide whether restrictive agreements made between businessmen may continue. A restriction is deemed to be contrary to the public interest unless the Court is satisfied that it is reasonably necessary or that its removal would be more harmful to the public than its retention. The first President of the Court was Mr Justice Devlin. For a hearing the Court is composed of one, two or three of the judges and two or more other members, and is therefore a mixed Court of judges and laymen. As the Minister said when introducing the bill in 1956, the decisions to be made were decisions not only of fact and law but of economic and social judgment. And so it proved to be. During the first six years of its hearings, the Court decided 26 major English cases ranging widely over different industries. During the first sixteen months, only one out of seven restrictions was upheld; during the next eighteen months, two out of nine were upheld; during the next two years, six out of ten were upheld.[12]

The second case decided by the Court was one of its most significant. In *Re Yarn Spinners Agreement*[13] the Court consisted of three High Court judges and four laymen and it was asked to consider an agreement under which the Yarn Spinners' Association asked its members to adopt prescribed minimum prices. The cotton industry for many years had been in recession because of competition from India, Pakistan, Japan and Hong Kong. The Court concluded that the effect of ending the agreement and so creating a free market would be to raise the general level of unemployment in eleven areas, in which about 100,000 employees (or about 70 per cent of the industry) were situated, from 4.3 per cent to 5.9 per cent; and in four of those areas from 5.2 per cent to 7.8 per cent. Put simply, the Court had to choose between this rise in the level of unemployment on the one hand, and the disadvantage of the higher price, the damage to the export trade, and the waste of national resources on the other. The Court decided that the agreement was contrary to the public interest and so accepted the consequence of a rise in unemployment.

Obviously that is a political judgment and the Court said things like: 'We are satisfied that the industry can and ought to be made smaller and more compact . . . We cannot see why price invasion is a bad thing or something which ought to be prevented; it is only one form of normal trade competition . . . Competition in quality is no doubt a benefit, but the removal of the restrictions would not prevent it.' And in a curious sentence the Court, having noted that the unemployment might cause great hardship, added: 'But we are clear that once we have reached a conclusion of fact, it is our duty to disregard the consequences of our findings.'

The use of judges in this way to make political and economic decisions was widely criticized in 1956. But by 1964 the Court was generally thought to have been successful. The Resale Prices Act of 1964 extended the Court's jurisdiction but during the debates in that year Lord Gardiner who was to become Lord Chancellor later that year expressed doubts about 'the increasing practice in the last ten years of employing Her Majesty's Judges to perform tasks other than their ordinary tasks'. He added, 'I am not quite clear whether Her Majesty's Judges have any special qualifications to determine what are really socio-economic questions, but they have done well'.[14] Lord Gardiner did not explain what he meant by this last phrase. Nevertheless doubts continued to be expressed about the wisdom of involving judges in the making of political decisions of this kind and this view was supported by those who believed that judicial purity, as they saw it, should be preserved. On the other hand it could be argued that the control of monopolies and restrictive practices by the courts has a long history. It may be that the operation of the Restrictive Practices Court provided some sort of precedent for the involvement of the judiciary in the highly political field of industrial relations.

INDUSTRIAL RELATIONS

Under the Industrial Courts Act of 1919[15] the Minister may set up a court of enquiry into a trade dispute. Since 1954, thirteen of such courts have been presided over by judges, normally with two experienced non-lawyers. Lord Pearson leads the field with five enquiries into disputes in the electricity supply, seamen's, civil air transport, steel, and port industries.[16] Lord Cameron follows with four: Ford's, port transport, printing, and building sites.[17] Lord Wilberforce presided over two enquiries into disputes in the electricity supply and coal industries;[18] Lord Morris into a shipbuilding and engineering dispute,[19] and Lord Evershed into a London docks dispute.[20]

These are far from being solely fact-finding enquiries. The terms of reference frequently require the court to have regard to the public interest or the national interest or the national economy or considerations like 'the need for an efficient and competitive' industry.[21] In one recent enquiry[22] into the electricity supply industry, Lord Wilberforce asked the Treasury to submit a memorandum on the significance of the dispute to the interests of the national economy and the Treasury responded with a document that argued for a progressive and substantial reduction in the levels of settlements.[23] This request from the court caused some difficulties as it was argued that the Government was seeking to impose its views and even a favoured solution of the dispute upon the court. Lord Wilberforce sought to rebut this but the request clearly, in the minds of some, showed that the court was not independent or impartial.

The status and function of these courts came into question during the most recent and one of the most critical of these enquiries, that presided over by Lord Wilberforce in 1972 into the dispute about miners' pay[24] which had led to a widespread stoppage of work. The extent to which the courts could become involved in the politics of such disputes had been shown a few years earlier when Lord Cameron presided over an enquiry into a dispute on London building sites.[25] The report then expressed the opinion that certain workmen should be eligible for re-employment if they sought it but not in any circumstances for election as shop stewards; and that other workmen should not be offered re-employment.

In the miners' dispute Lord Wilberforce became deeply enmeshed in job evaluation, the social and physical conditions in the pits and, above all, the need to produce a settlement under which the miners would go back to work. Lord Wilberforce discovered that there were two factors in any possible wage increase. One was the periodic factor – that wages did increase from time to time, and the other was what he called the adjustment factor which meant that a time might come in any industry when a distortion or trend had to be recognized as such for correction. 'The existence of these two quite separate factors' said the report, 'appears to have been overlooked until the present Enquiry brought it to light.' If a large increase could not be paid for by the National Coal Board then the Government should meet it.

The *Economist* referred to the device of 'calling in a

High Court judge to write incredible economic nonsense',[26] but whatever view is taken of the justice or the wisdom of the report which recommended a considerable wage increase and which formed the basis of the settlement, the impression given was that the Government had set up this enquiry to produce a report which would enable them to yield to the miners' claim without total loss of face.

Under other legislation, less formal committees may be set up to enquire into trade disputes and in the 1960s Lord Devlin produced three reports on the port industry[27] and Lord Cameron reported on a dispute concerning bank employees.[28]

In 1962, the Royal Commission on the Press recommended that there should be set up a Press Amalgamations Court, like the Restrictive Practices Court, consisting of judges of the High Court and lay members appointed on the recommendation of the Lord Chancellor after consultation with the Trades Union Congress and the Press Council.[29] Lord Hailsham, then a Minister, was doubtful about the value of the idea as he thought that the question of the public interest in a proposed amalgamation (which the Court would have to consider) was 'not justiciable'. He went on to point out 'the danger of getting the judiciary into politics' especially as newspapers were often linked to political parties. The primary concern of the judiciary, said Lord Hailsham, must be 'to retain the respect of the public for their independence – which involves not merely their real independence of mind, but also the belief which the public can have that they are seen to be independent in every respect.'[30] Eight years later these considerations did not apparently deter Lord Hailsham (then Lord Chancellor) from supporting the setting up of the National Industrial Relations Court (NIRC).

When in 1970 the Minister was introducing legislation in the Commons which created the NIRC he said that the NIRC's existence showed 'in fact as well as in symbol' that the provisions of the Bill[31] would not be arbitrarily implemented by the Secretary of State of the day but would 'depend on the rule of law'. The Court, he said (inaccurately), would be 'something new in British justice' and would consist of judges and laymen sitting together.[32]

Many kinds of dispute arising out of industrial relations could find their way to the NIRC which, because of its status as a superior court of record and the powers given it by statute, was able to order the payment of fines and, if that or any other of its orders was disregarded, could imprison for contempt The application of that sanction led to the involvement of the ordinary courts. Here I am concerned to emphasize that the NIRC was required by the legislation under which it operated to make decisions which were likely to lead, and did in fact lead, to considerable and widespread political protest.

Whether the NIRC always acted with the greatest wisdom may be debatable. But its failure was due not primarily to the way it performed its functions, but to the nature of those functions. Many people doubted whether the issues before the Restrictive Practices Court were justiciable. What the NIRC was required to do was to make binding decisions, and to see that they were enforced in the context of dispute between trade unions, individual workmen, employers, and employers' federations. This, as many said at the time, was not a function which judges and courts could perform successfully.

Now under the Employment Protection Act of 1975 an Appeal Tribunal has been set up consisting of judges, and of others having special knowledge or experience of industrial relations, either as representatives of employers or as representatives of workers. So in structure, if not in other ways, this Tribunal is similar to the NIRC. It can hear appeals from tribunals under or by virtue of the Equal Pay Act 1970, the Sex Discrimination Act 1975 and others, as well as the Employment Protection Act itself. It is a somewhat curious body in that much of its jurisdiction is to hear appeals on questions of law, for which the lay members might appear unfitted. Perhaps we are seeing, as an evolution (the origins of which can be traced to the nineteenth century), the emergence of a genuine hybrid tribunal, in which case to suggest that this body is a further example of the use of judges for extra-judicial activities is only one way to describe it. It could also be said to be an example of the developed use of experienced laymen to assist in the determination of disputes.

NORTHERN IRELAND

The first involvement of judges, acting outside their courts, in Northern Ireland was in 1969 when the Governor appointed Lord Cameron to lead a commission of enquiry into disturbances.[33] Then in 1971 Sir Edmund Compton (not a judge but the former Parliamentary Commissioner for Administration) chaired an enquiry into allegations of physical brutality by the security forces. Sir Edmund found there had been cases of physical ill-treatment such as wall-standing, hooding, noise, deprivation of sleep, and diets of bread and water. The Home Secretary rejected any suggestion that the methods authorized for inter-rogation contained any element of cruelty but he appointed three Privy Councillors to consider those methods. One was Lord Parker (who had just retired as Lord Chief Justice) and another was Lord Gardiner (who had been Lord Chancellor from 1964 to 1970). Lord Parker and the third Privy Councillor (Mr J. A. Boyd-Carpenter) concluded that these methods, subject to proper safeguards, and limiting the occasions on which and the degree to which they could be applied, conformed to the authority given. Lord Gardiner said that they were secret, illegal, not morally justifiable and alien to the traditions of what he believed still to be the greatest democracy in the world. The disagreement was wide.[34]

In April 1972, two reports were published. Lord Widgery (who had succeeded Lord Parker as Lord Chief Justice) had been appointed as a one-man tribunal of enquiry to enquire into the events of 'Bloody Sunday' which led to

13 civilian deaths in Londonderry. This tribunal was set up under the Tribunals of Enquiry (Evidence) Act 1921 the procedure of which is designed to elicit facts. The line between matters of fact and opinions deduced from facts is not always easy to draw. Lord Widgery spoke about the justifiability of decisions taken by army commanders and soldiers, about actions which, he concluded, did 'not require censure', and in using such language caused dispute and argument about the nature of his findings.[35]

In the meantime Mr Justice Scarman had since 1969 been enquiring with two others into the violence and civil disturbances of that year. This tribunal also operated under the Act of 1921 and its report was substantial. It investigated a large number of incidents and drew conclusions about fault and responsibility. It assessed the social cost in terms of deaths, personal injuries, damage to property, damage to licensed premises, intimidation and displacement of persons.[36]

At the end of 1972 a Commission under the chairmanship of Lord Diplock reported on the legal procedures to deal with terrorist activities in Northern Ireland. It concluded that the main obstacle to dealing efficiently with terrorist crime in the regular courts of justice was intimidation of would-be prosecution witnesses. It recommended that trials of scheduled terrorist offences should be conducted without a jury; that members of the armed services should be given power to arrest and to detain for up to four hours to establish identity; that bail should not normally be granted; that the onus of proof as to the possession of firearms and explosives should in certain circumstances be shifted to the accused; and that the rules about the admissibility as evidence of confessions and signed statements should be relaxed.[37]

That Commission led to the passing of the Northern Ireland (Emergency Provisions) Act 1973. In 1974 Lord Gardiner was appointed chairman of a Committee to consider what provisions and powers, consistent to the maximum extent practicable in the circumstances with the preservation of civil liberties and human rights, were required to deal with terrorism and subversion in Northern Ireland, including provisions for the administration of justice; and to examine the working of the Act of 1973. The Committee reported early in 1975,[38] and made a large number of recommendations, some endorsing the Diplock Commission and the Act, others being critical and proposing amendments to the law. In particular, it proposed the ending of detention without trial as soon as was politically possible, and it condemned as a serious mistake the establishment of a 'special category' for convicted prisoners claiming political motivation.

So from the beginning of 1972 there have been involved in five major enquiries relating to Northern Ireland a former Lord Chancellor (twice), a present and a former Lord Chief Justice, a Lord of Appeal, and a High Court judge. On one occasion, two of these were seen to be in open disagreement about the legitimacy and desirability of actions taken by the authorities; on another occasion, one of these was set up, in effect, to review recommendations made by another. It may be that a judge is well qualified to conduct enquiries to establish what took place on particular occasions. But it is impossible for him in his findings not to interpret events. He must draw deductions about what he thinks took place from the evidence that is presented to him. And so he will be involved in political controversy and, in circumstances like those prevailing in Northern Ireland, inevitably accused of bias, of whitewashing, of serving certain political masters. These accusations may be wholly untrue but they will be made to an extent not paralleled by criticism of any judgment he may make from the bench of the regular courts.

LEGISLATIVE PROCESS

Finally, the most senior judges sit in the House of Lords[39] and may take part in its legislative and other activities. Lords of Appeal in Ordinary – Law Lords – receive life baronies on appointment unless they are already ennobled. A survey has been made[40] of the 26 judges who were active Law Lords during the period 1952-68 together with two Lord Chief Justices, two Masters of the Rolls and one President of what was then the Probate, Divorce and Admiralty Division. The authors of the survey say that there was very little 'in the way of political activism' on the part of the Law Lords whose contribution to debates on bills was largely that of acting as 'resident technical consultants to the legislature on legal points' and it seems that those with records of overt political affiliation do not speak more than others.

While participating Law Lords agreed with one another more frequently than they disagreed, the authors of the survey list thirteen items between 1956 and 1967 where there was a substantial measure of agreement and of these several were not matters of technical law. They included capital punishment, artificial insemination, adultery, the minimum age for the death penalty, corporal punishment of young offenders, and disputes concerning majority verdicts, suspended sentences and parole. In one recent debate, five Law Lords, in an unprecedented way, spoke against a legislative proposal which provided that in assessing damages payable to a widow on the death of her husband, her remarriage or prospects of remarriage should not be taken into account. Two other Law Lords participated and all the Law Lords with two exceptions attended the debate on 6 May 1971. 'In the face of almost certain defeat in the Lobby,' say Blom-Cooper and Drewry, 'the Law Lords, as decorously as they were able, withdrew their amendment and retired once more into their judicial shells.'[41]

Where technical law ends and political controversy begins is not always easy to determine. It is clear, however, that Law Lords while for the most part restricting themselves to the obviously technical are not averse from speaking on social questions like capital punishment, the treatment of offenders and adultery. They do occasionally assume the role of 'self-appointed guardians of the nation's conscience'.[42]

A well-known example from earlier in this century of a Law Lord speaking on a political matter in the House of Lords arose when Lord Carson in 1921 strongly attacked the proposal to establish an Irish Free State. His right to do so was challenged by Lord Chancellor Birkenhead and defended by former Lord Chancellor Finlay during a debate in 1922 on Law Lords and party politics.[43]

In 1963, Lord Hodson, already well-known for his judicial views on matrimonial matters, strongly opposed provisions in Mr Leo Abse's Matrimonial Causes and Reconciliation Bill. He spoke once during the second reading debate, spoke or intervened 13 times in committee, once on report, and once on third reading.[44] And Lord Hodson was concerned primarily with the substantive merits and demerits of the Bill, not with its legal technicalities.

But more dramatic and more political was Lord Salmon's contribution in 1975 to the debates on the Government's controversial Trade Union and Labour Relations (Amendment) Bill. He said:

> We cannot shut our eyes to the fact that there are groups, very small numerically but extremely cohesive and tenacious, who have infiltrated the unions with the intention of seizing power if they can. Their objects and ideas are entirely different from those of the trade unions, which we all know and respect. Their avowed purpose is to wreck the Social Contract and the democratic system under which we live. Their ethos derives from foreign lands where individual liberty is dead, and where the courts and trade unions are mere tools of the Executive, to do its will.[45]

The argument is familiar – Lord Gordon-Walker said he had heard it for 40 years – but, even more, it is a political argument. Lord Salmon clearly felt strongly and spoke in the name of freedom and democracy. He posed the question whether the disadvantage of a judge speaking on matters which in one form or another – such as unfair dismissal from employment or from a trade union – might well come before him when he was on the bench was outweighed by the advantage of hearing his views or by the argument that he should not be prevented, by convention or otherwise, from speaking in Parliament on such a matter.[46]

If one believes that judges can and should be politically neutral when they are on the judicial bench, then their involvement in such highly political questions as restrictive practices, industrial relations and Northern Ireland, is to be regretted. But if one does not believe that the pure doctrine of political neutrality can be or is applicable to judges in their courts, then their involvement in outside political affairs appears less regrettable. If it is accepted that judges on the bench already display common characteristics and common attitudes when they are dealing with political cases (see below, p. 193) then it is difficult to argue that their judgments are seriously contaminated by their extra-judicial activities. If we swallow the camel, we should not strain at the gnat.

The falseness arises when judges are put forward to preside over enquiries which are inherently political in character (such as any dispute connected with the disorders and killings in Northern Ireland or with large-scale industrial disputes) on the ground that their participation will ensure neutrality. When this is done and when subsequently it comes to be perceived by large numbers of people that the neutrality is a sham, then damage is done to the judicial system.

To say that the neutrality is a sham does not mean that judges act dishonestly. It means that if a judge is sent to preside over an enquiry in Northern Ireland or into a nationwide strike by power workers, he can do no more than any other intelligent man. He will try to make allowance for his own prejudices to the extent that he knows

51

them and he will try to produce a report which will leave matters nearer to an agreed solution than they were before he arrived. But if the myth of his neutrality and objectivity, *because he is a judge*, is paraded, its exploding will make more difficult the proper performance on the bench of all members of the judiciary.

The purpose of this book is to look at the ways in which judges of the High Court, the Court of Appeal, and the House of Lords have in recent years dealt with political cases which have come before them. By political I mean those cases which arise out of controversial legislation or controversial action initiated by public authorities, or which touch important moral or social issues.

When people like the members of the judiciary, broadly homogeneous in character, are faced with such political situations, they act in broadly similar ways. It will be part of my argument to suggest that behind these actions lies a unifying attitude of mind, a political position, which is primarily concerned to protect and conserve certain values and institutions. This does not mean that the judiciary inevitably and invariably supports what Governments do, or even what Conservative Governments do, though that is the natural inclination. Individually, judges may support the Conservative or the Labour or the Liberal Parties. Collectively, in their function and by their nature, they are neither Tories nor Socialists nor Liberals. They are protectors and conservators of what has been, of the relationships and interests on which, *in their view*, our society is founded. It is as difficult to imagine the judiciary in the United Kingdom handing down judgments like those sometimes handed down by the Supreme Court of the United States, based on radical and reforming principles, as it would be to imagine such judgments being handed down by the Supreme Court of the Soviet Union.

NOTES

1. See T. J. Cartwright, *Royal Commissions & Departmental Committees in Britain*; see also G. Rhodes, *Committees of Inquiry*.

2. See Cartwright, *op cit*, p. 72. His other groups are civil service, retired central government; other government (active or retired); legal profession; business, finance, industry; medical profession; trade unions; other: no information.

3. See Scottish Law Commission: Memorandum no. 32 incorporating also an earlier memorandum.

4. 367 H. L. Deb. col. 837 (27 January 1976).

5. Cmnd 7616.

6. Cmnd 350.

7. Cmnd 718.

8. Cmnd 2009.

9. H. C. 553 of 1966-7.

10. See below, p. 47; see generally Cmnd 3121.

11. H. C. 133 of 1971-2.

12. See R. B. Stevens and B. S. Yamey, *The Restrictive Practices Court*. (See now the Restrictive Practices Court Act 1976.)

13. [1959] 1 W. L. R. 154.

14. 258 H. L. Deb. col. 835, 836.

15. I was helped by being able to read an unpublished thesis for MSc (Econ.) by David Cockburn (1972).

16. Cmnd 2361, 3025, 3211, 3551, 3754, 4429.

17. Cmnd 131, 510, 3184, 3396.

18. Cmnd 4954, 4903.

19. Cmnd 9084, 9085.

20. Cmnd 9302, 9310.

21. See Cmnd 3025 – the industry was shipping.

22. See Cmnd 4594.

23. See Cmnd 4579.

24. See Cmnd 4903.

25. Cmnd 3396.

26. 26 February 1972.

27. Cmnd 2523, 2734, 3104.

28. Cmnd 2202.

29. Cmnd 1811 paras 337-49.

30. 250 H. L. Deb. col. 938-9.

31. This became the Industrial Relations Act 1971.

32. 808 H. C. Deb. col. 982.

33. Cmnd 532.

34. Cmnd 4901 (March 1972).

35. H. C. 220 of 1971-2.

36. Cmnd 566.
37. Cmnd 5185.
38. Cmnd 5847.
39. I.e., the Upper House of Parliament.
40. L. Blom-Cooper and G. Drewry, *Final Appeal*, c. 10.
41. *Ibid.*, p. 215.
42. *Ibid.*, p. 204.
43. 49 H. L. Deb. col. 931-73.
44. 250 H. L. Deb. col. 401-5, 1537, 1538-43; vol. 251 col. 1553-5, 1560, 1561, 1564, 1578-9, 1591-4, 1595, 1596, 1597, 1600; vol. 252 col. 419-20, 430.
45. 358 H. L. Deb. col. 27.
46. For other, earlier, examples (mostly on more legal questions) see Shetreet, *op cit*, pp. 257-8, 345-7.

PART TWO

Cases

*The Court's position had not been made any easier by
suggestions that it was possible for the Government
to influence its decisions. The Court was surprised
that those suggestions should have been made, and the
Court owed it to its members and to all concerned to
make it clear that no attempt had been made by anyone
directly or indirectly, otherwise than in open court,
to influence its decision.*

(Sir John Donaldson, President of the National Industrial
Relations Court in *Midland Cold Storage Ltd v. Turner
and Others* as reported in *The Times* newspaper 28 July
1972.)

Chapter 3: Industrial relations

From the middle ages, Parliament has been concerned with the problems, central to the national economy, of productivity and the control of wages. And, for hundreds of years, workers who were thought to be failing in their duties were subjected to imprisonment and other penalties.

The use of the penal law against workers, especially when it involves imprisonment, or the possibility of imprisonment, is one of the most persistent sources of conflict between labour and management, and between labour and Governments. Parliament legislated extensively against the combination of workers but the judges also, through their power of interpreting statutes and of making and extending the common law, were a powerful source of constraint on the emerging trade union movement in the industrial society of the nineteenth century. Two outstanding characteristics of labour law during the second half of that century were the intermittent recognition by politicians in Government and Parliament that control of trade unionism by the imposition of penalties was of doubtful efficacy; and the recurrent attempts by the courts to preserve the penal method.[1]

Statutes of 1859, 1871 and 1875, were designed to relieve trade unions of criminal liability, especially for conspiracy. Specifically, the Conspiracy and Protection of Property Act 1875 provided that an agreement by two or more persons to do or procure to be done any act in contemplation or furtherance of a trade dispute should not be a criminal conspiracy unless the act itself was punishable as a crime. So the right to strike was established.

The last decade of the nineteenth century saw the development of a considerable antipathy to trade unionism among influential public opinion. This was in part due to the emergence of New Unionism which sought to organize unskilled workers. Professor Saville has written that the old unions 'were able to rely upon the skill of their members as a crucial bargaining weapon' but 'the new unionists were at all times, even in years of good trade, subject to the pressures of an over-stocked labour market'. So 'the employers, too, in the semi- and unskilled trades were more uncompromising than their fellows in industries where unionism had long been established.' The industrial offensive against the trade unions in the early years of the 1890s was 'most successful against the dockers, the seamen and the casual trades' but all the New Unions lost heavily in membership.[2]

It is against the background of this offensive that the judicial decisions of 1896[3]-1901 must be seen. Although the right to strike had been established, some of the judges were not to be so easily defeated. In addition to the crime of conspiracy, there was the civil wrong (or tort) of conspiracy, consisting of an agreement which has been acted on and which is made in order to attain either an unlawful object or a lawful object by unlawful means. It was to this that some judges turned their attention.

In *Allen v. Flood*[4] a dispute arose between the ironworkers' union and woodworkers, the former objecting to certain work being done by the latter. Ironworkers told one of their officials that they would stop working if the woodworkers were continued in employment. The official informed the employers accordingly and the employers lawfully dismissed the woodworkers who then brought an action against the official.

The case was first argued in December 1895 before seven members of the House of Lords[5] including Lord Chancellor Halsbury, and a former Lord Chancellor, Herschell. 'From the very beginning,' says Professor Heuston, 'Lord Halsbury took a view strongly adverse to the position of the trade union and expressed his firm opinion that the plaintiffs . . . were entitled to damages for an interference with their right to work. It was also clear, however, that on this point he would be unable to carry with him a majority of his colleagues.' Apparently, Halsbury then 'conceived the idea that the case should be re-argued before an enlarged body of Law Lords and that, in addition, the House should adopt once more the practice of summoning the High Court judges to advise', a practice generally thought to be obsolete. Lord Herschell was angered by this idea and, says Professor Heuston, 'the High Court judges at that time, many of whom were Halsbury's own appointments, were not on the whole notable for progressive views on social or industrial matters.'[6]

Between 25 March and 2 April 1897 the case was re-argued before the original seven Law Lords and two others. Of the eight High Court judges who attended, and gave their 'opinions', six agreed with Lord Halsbury and two disagreed. But when the nine Law Lords delivered their judgments in December 1897, Lord Halsbury's views were supported by only two of his colleagues, with Lord Herschell and five others in the opposing majority. So the trade unions remained protected.

Then in 1901, in *Quinn v. Leathem*,[7] the effect of that decision was reversed. For many years, L. supplied a butcher with meat. The trade union sought to persuade L. not to employ non-union men. When this failed, the union instructed their members working for the butcher that, if he continued to buy L.'s meat, they were to cease work. So the butcher took no more meat from L. who brought an action against the union officials for conspiracy to injure him. The House of Lords decided in his favour.

In *Quinn v. Leathem* five Law Lords delivered judgments and they were unanimous in deciding against the union officials. In addition to Lord Halsbury, two of them had taken part in *Allen v. Flood* where they had been in the majority. Now they supported the Lord Chancellor. The distinctions drawn between the two cases were primarily that in *Allen v. Flood* there was no conspiring between two or more persons (as there was in *Quinn v.*

Leathem) and that in *Allen v. Flood* the purpose of the defendant was to promote his own trade interest whereas in *Quinn v. Leathem* the purpose of the defendants was to injure the plaintiff in his trade rather than legitimately to advance their own interests. From the trade unionists' viewpoint the effect of *Quinn v. Leathem* was seriously to curtail their power to operate in ways which would strengthen the working class movement against employers. This was thought by trade unionists to be inconsistent with the leading decision of ten years before which had protected employers' associations from conspiracy on the ground that the acts had been done 'with the lawful object of protecting and extending their trade and increasing their profits' without employing unlawful means, although the consequence had been to injure their competitors.[8]

These judicial decisions caused great political upheaval and resulted in the passing of the Trade Disputes Act 1906 which followed the same pattern as the Act of 1875, protecting trade unions from actions for civil conspiracy if the acts were done in furtherance or contemplation of a trade dispute.

Another struggle centred on trade union funds. In law, property may be held either by a natural person, or by a number of such persons, or by an incorporated body such as a company. Trade unions fell into the second of these groups, but, because of their large and fluctuating membership and because of certain provisions in the Trade Union Act 1871, it was assumed that it was impracticable to bring actions against them so as to make their funds liable. In 1900 a dispute arose because it was said that the Taff Vale Railway Company had victimized a trade unionist who led a wage demand. The House of Lords held that trade unions could be sued, in effect, for losses sustained by employers as a consequence of strike action.[9] Lord Halsbury gave one of the five unanimous judgments. As Professor Heuston says, the decision left 'a legacy of suspicion and mistrust . . . to poison relations between the courts and the unions for many years.' He adds: 'One of Baldwin's favourite themes was the folly of this *Taff Vale* decision: 'The Conservatives can't talk of class-war: They started it,' he would remark to G. M. Young.[10]

But it is not clear that Baldwin was referring to the House of Lords' decision. G. M. Young said that Baldwin's theme was 'the gross and almost irreparable error which, under the vehement guidance of Lord Chancellor Halsbury, the Conservative Government had made in 1901'[11] and Young goes on to say that in Baldwin's view the Tory party (that is, the Government) should at once, by passing an Act of Parliament, have restored the position intended by the Tory legislation of 1875.[12] Baldwin's comment seems therefore to refer to the political failure of the Tory Government to reverse the *Taff Vale* decision rather than to the decision itself and we are left to wonder whether Halsbury's 'vehement guidance' was exercised over his fellow judges or over his colleagues in the Cabinet. Certainly his judgment in the Lords was the reverse of vehement and consisted of one substantive sentence of fifty moderate words. So perhaps we have here an example of a Lord Chancellor publicly delivering judgment in a case and then privately urging his political colleagues not to reverse it by legislation.

The *Taff Vale* decision was a serious blow to trade unionism. The law had seemed 'so clearly settled to the contrary', wrote Lord Asquith, that 'public opinion was unprepared for any such decision.'[13] Liberal opinion strongly favoured its reversal. This was effectively carried through by the strong Liberal Government elected in 1906 in the Trade Disputes Act of that year.

A few years later, the judiciary again intervened, this time by invoking the doctrine of *ultra vires*. This doctrine applies mainly to public authorities exercising statutory powers and to companies registered under the Companies Acts to pursue certain objects described in their constitutions. If powers or objects are exceeded, action can be brought to restrain those authorities or companies. Trade unions had for some time been supporting candidates for the House of Commons and spending union funds for this purpose. In 1909, a member of the Amalgamated Society of Railway Servants successfully challenged this practice.[14] This of course was also a severe blow to the emerging Labour Party and again the politicians had to try to restore what had been understood to be the position by passing the Trade Union Act 1913.[15]

For much of the interwar period, the judges seemed to withdraw from the conflict or, when asked to intervene, tended to adopt a neutral position. Indeed, such decisions as were made were markedly more generous in their recognition of the legitimacy of the purposes of trade unions. Moreover, during the 1930s, employers did not need to seek the help of the courts, the unions being in a weak condition. As we shall see, judicial intervention was not noticeably restrained at this time in other political cockpits.

THE GENERAL STRIKE

Nevertheless the general strike of 1926 gave rise to one case in the courts and a group of incidents seemed to show some curious connections between the courts and the politicians. On Thursday 6 May 1926 (the third day of the strike) Sir John Simon MP spoke in the House of Commons. Then known as a former Attorney-General and a former Home Secretary, Sir John was a Liberal MP who still perhaps had hopes of leading his party in the future. He argued that the general strike was not a strike at all because it was unlawful as the workmen had 'terminated their engagements' without giving due notice to their employers. The decision of the General Council of the Trades Union Congress to call out everybody was not, he said, a lawful act and every workman who obeyed it had broken the law. The general strike was 'a novel and an utterly illegal proceeding'. Thus every railwayman on strike was 'personally liable to be sued in the County Court for damages'. Sir John went further and said that every trade union leader who had advised and promoted the strike was 'liable in damages to the uttermost farthing of his personal possessions'. He then emphasized in what he called 'a perfectly dogmatic statement' that no trade unionist who refused to obey the order of his union to strike would lose any benefits payable under a rule of the union because the order would be unlawful. 'It cannot be too widely and plainly known,' said Sir John, 'that there is no court in this country which would ever construe such a rule as meaning that the man would forfeit his benefits if he is asked to do that which is wrong and illegal.[16]

The following Monday (10th) the Cabinet met at 4.30 p.m. and agreed that the Prime Minister (Mr Baldwin) should arrange for a question and answer in the House of Commons the next day to the following effect:

Question Does the Government intend to deal with the position of the Trades Unions?
Answer The Government are not now contemplating any modification in existing trades union legislation, but they are considering the desirability of making clear what they believe to be now the law, namely, that a general strike is illegal.

That Monday evening Sir Henry Slesser, who had been Solicitor-General in the Labour Government of 1924, replied in the House (against the wishes of his leader Ramsay MacDonald) to correct what he believed to be 'an erroneous view of the law'. He deplored Simon's introduction of 'highly debatable' questions of law which, he said, should be discussed in the Law Courts and not in Parliament.[17] Sir John responded at 6 p.m. the next afternoon[18] and was able strongly to buttress his arguments with quotations from a judgment delivered that very morning by Mr Justice Astbury in the Chancery Division of the High Court. When the Cabinet met (also at 6 p.m.), their attention was drawn to this judgment. The Prime Minister informed his colleagues that, as a result of a consultation with the Earl of Birkenhead, a Cabinet colleague, 'following the receipt of certain information'[19] he had earlier decided not to implement the Cabinet decision to arrange for a question and answer in the House of Commons.

The case arose because the National Sailors' and Firemen's Union did not support the strike but their Tower Hill branch passed a resolution calling out their members in support of the TUC. The Union asked for a declaration that the secretary and delegates of the branch were not entitled to call out their members and for an injunction to restrain them from doing so. In the course of his judgment, Mr Justice Astbury said:

> The so-called general strike called by the Trades Union Congress Council is illegal, and persons inciting or taking part in it are not protected by the Trade Disputes Act 1906. No trade dispute has been alleged or shown to exist in any of the unions affected, except in the miners' case, and no trade dispute does or can exist between the Trades Union Congress on the one hand and the Government and the nation on the other.

Astbury went on to say that no member of the Union could lose his trade union benefits by refusing to obey unlawful orders. An injunction was issued.[20]

It seems that the case was first heard by Astbury on 6 May, on the evening of which day Sir John Simon made his first speech, declared the general strike illegal, argued that strikers were liable to pay damages, and referred to the protection of non-strikers' benefits. Then, the day after Sir Henry Slesser's attack, Astbury delivered his judgment which strongly supported Sir John's position and provided judicial authority for Sir John's second speech that same evening. It is difficult to believe that the judge and the politician were not sharing their thoughts on this matter. It seems likely that they knew one another well. Astbury had been a fellow Liberal MP for four years having been first returned at the same time as Simon during the Liberal victory of 1906; and he was made a judge in 1913 during Simon's five-year period as Solicitor-General and then Attorney-General.

Opinions differ greatly about the importance of Simon's speeches and Astbury's judgment.[21] It is said that Astbury claimed more than once that his contribution had saved the nation. And, on one view, the TUC leaders were genuinely alarmed at the prospect of imprisonment. But there were undoubtedly more important factors affecting the decision of the TUC to call off the general strike on 12 May.

As I have said, the courts were not much involved in disputes affecting trade unions during the 1930s or for some years after 1945. But the 1960s gave rise to certain assumptions about the nature and the power of trade unions which, true or false, have coloured and affected the attitudes of the middle classes and, in consequence, the policies of the Conservative, Labour and Liberal Parties. Once again, the judges have become central figures in these political issues.

PICKETING

Picketing is a practice which stands uneasily across the boundary, as variously interpreted, of legal and illegal action. It can become conduct likely to cause a breach of the peace, or obstruction, or even assault. The Conspiracy and Protection of Property Act 1875 restated the criminal offence of 'watching or besetting' but excluded from that activity 'attending at or near the house or place where a person resides, or works, or carries on business, or happens to be . . . in order merely to obtain or communicate information'. But in *Lyons v. Wilkins*[22] the Court of Appeal had decided against the officers of a trade union who, having ordered a strike against the plaintiffs and against S (who made goods for the plaintiffs only), organized pickets to seek to persuade work-people not to work for the plaintiffs. That, said Lindley L. J., was not merely obtaining or communicating information. It was putting pressure on the plaintiffs by persuading people not to enter their employment. And that was illegal. It was further decided that such watching and besetting might be a nuisance at common law and illegal on that ground also. Once again the legislature reversed the courts and by the Trade Disputes Act 1906 made picketing lawful if in contemplation or furtherance of a trade dispute and if the purpose was peacefully obtaining or communicating information or 'peacefully persuading any person to work or abstain from working'.

The interpretation of the law remained contentious. During a trade dispute in 1960, a police officer found two pickets standing at the front entrance of a factory, four standing at the back entrance and ten or twelve outside the back entrance. The officer told the defendant three times that he considered two pickets at each entrance were sufficient but the defendant, persisting in his intention to join the pickets, 'pushed gently past' the police officer, 'was gently arrested', and was charged with obstructing the police in the execution of their duty. The Divisional Court held that he was properly convicted on the ground that the police officer had reasonable grounds for anticipating that a breach of the peace was a real possibility.[23] In *Tynan v. Balmer*[24] (1966) forty pickets in a continuous circle around a factory (which had the effect of sealing off the highway) were held not to be legalized by the Act of 1906 because their action was a nuisance at common law and an unreasonable use of the highway. In 1972, a strike picket held a placard in front of a vehicle on a highway, urging the driver not to work at a site nearby and preventing him from proceeding along the highway. The picket was charged with obstruction of the highway although the whole incident lasted for not more than nine minutes. The House of Lords upheld the prosecution.[25] The following year, a police cordon prevented pickets from approaching a coach carrying workers out of a site.

The defendant was involved in a scuffle with a constable and was successfully charged with obstructing him in the execution of his duty.[26] The result of these cases was greatly to limit the right to picket. They enlarged the scope within which the police could prevent picketing and they greatly narrowed the scope within which picketing could lawfully be undertaken.[27]

Moreover, the use by the courts of these common law devices of obstruction, breach of the peace and nuisance is difficult to legislate against as the essential purpose (which before the 1960s had been more or less achieved with police co-operation) is to permit 'reasonable' picketing, including the right to accost for a short period within which arguments can be advanced, without putting persons in fear or to immoderate inconvenience.

'The attendance', said counsel for the defendant in *Hunt v. Broome* 'is for the purpose of peacefully persuading a man not to work so the attendance must be in a position where the persuasion can be carried out; otherwise its purpose is frustrated . . . Attendance for the purpose of peaceful persuasion is what is protected by the Act . . . not mere attendance, standing with banners; the attendance is for oral communication.'[28]

As the courts presently interpret the law this purpose is often difficult and sometimes impossible to achieve. It is also true that the right to picket may be abused.

THE RIGHT TO STRIKE

In 1964 the House of Lords in *Rookes v. Barnard*[29] delivered a judgment which seemed like a return to the early heady days of the century. R worked for BOAC with whom his union had an agreement that all workers should be union members. In 1955 R left the union after a disagreement with union members. Two local union members, and a district union official employed by the union, threatened BOAC that labour would be withdrawn if R were not removed within 3 days as required by a resolution passed at a members' meeting. Such a strike would have been a breach of contract by each member. BOAC gave R long notice and lawfully discharged him. R sued the two members and the official for conspiracy.

Under the Trade Disputes Act 1906 no action for conspiracy would lie unless the act would be unlawful if done by a person alone. So the Law Lords considered whether a threat to strike could be 'unlawful' in this sense. And they held it could be.

This decision was seen by trade unionists as a direct attack on the right to strike. The Law Lords certainly seemed to stretch themselves to arrive at their conclusion. Lord Devlin, for example, could find 'nothing to differentiate a threat of a breach of contract from a threat of physical violence'. It was a time when strikes were being blamed for most of the country's ills, and Lord Hodson said: 'The injury and suffering caused by strike action is very often widespread as well as devastating and a threat to strike would be expected to be certainly no less serious than a threat of violence.' Once again the politicians had to seek to reverse their Lordships' decision and passed the Trade Disputes Act 1965.

INDUCING BREACH OF CONTRACT

In 1952, certain drivers and loaders told Bowaters Ltd, the paper suppliers, that they might not be prepared to deliver paper to the plaintiffs who were printers and publishers. Bowaters told the plaintiffs and they brought an action against officers of the unions to which the drivers and loaders belonged. The Court of Appeal held that the evidence did not establish that there had been any direct procurement by the defendants of any wrongful acts by the drivers or loaders or that the latter had committed any wrongful acts; also that there was no evidence of any actual knowledge by the defendants of any contract between Bowaters and the plaintiffs. So the plaintiffs lost their action.[30]

In 1964, the House of Lords considered a case in which a union were met by a refusal of a company to negotiate with them on terms and conditions of service although they organized the majority of the men concerned, being watermen in the Port of London. Another union organized the minority. So the first union issued instructions that none of their men would man, service or tow empty barges belonging to the company. The company owned and hired out barges but did not employ any of the union men, but their action meant that barges were not returned and so the company's business came to a standstill. The company brought an action against the union officials. The House of Lords found for the company on the ground that the union had knowingly induced breaches of the hiring contract and their members' contracts of employment. Most importantly, their Lordships decided that there was, on the facts, no trade dispute within the meaning of the Trade Disputes Act 1906 because the basis of the embargo was trade-union rivalry.[31]

This attitude of the courts was strengthened by the decision of the Court of Appeal in *Torquay Hotel v. Cousins*.[32] Union members picketed the Torbay Hotel, cutting off fuel oil supplies, and later, when the manager of the plaintiffs' hotel was reported as having called for a stand against the union, picketed that hotel with the same result. The union also told an alternative oil supplier not to supply the plaintiff hotel. The Court of Appeal held that as the plaintiffs employed no union members the union's actions were not in furtherance of a trade dispute and injunctions were issued against the union. As Professor Wedderburn has observed, the result of this decision could be that where an association of employers is fighting off a trade union, it may be able to 'keep its smaller members in the front line and avoid any of its bigger members being parties to the dispute'.[33] The trade unions' 'golden formula' of action 'in furtherance of a trade dispute' looks weaker as a protection than it did.

No wonder that, in 1968, a member of the Royal Commission on Trade Unions and Employers' Associations wrote: [34]

A thing that worried me all through the deliberations . . . was this: supposing we made all the right recommendations and supposing the Government gave effect to them all in legislation, how long would it be before the judges turned everything upside down?

INDUSTRIAL RELATIONS ACT 1971

But the most dramatic judicial intervention was yet to come. In 1971 was passed the Industrial Relations Act. This measure of a Conservative Government was strongly opposed, in and out of Parliament, by the trade union movement and the Labour Party. It established the National Industrial Relations Court (NIRC) presided over by Sir John Donaldson, formerly a judge of the High Court. The NIRC had wide jurisdiction to consider complaints arising under the Act, to impose penalties, and to punish those who disregarded its orders.

In recent years, the amount of work available for dockworkers has drastically declined because of the growing practice of loading and unloading goods in containers at depots outside the port areas. From mid-1971, the Transport and General Workers' Union authorized the practice of selective 'blacking' of the goods carried by certain road haulier firms to ports. When the Act of 1971 came into force in February 1972, the union became liable to complaints and penalties for this blacking. The first complaint was made on 23 March 1972 and the NIRC ordered the union, its officers, servants and agents to refrain from certain specific blacking. The union's officers advised their shop stewards to obey this order but the advice was rejected. On 29 March the NIRC found the union in wilful contempt of the order and, following subsequent complaints, imposed fines totalling £55,000.[35]

On 13 June the Court of Appeal decided that the union was not accountable for its shop stewards and set aside the fines.[36] But the next day the NIRC ordered three London dockers who had defied an order against blacking made on 12 June to be committed to prison for contempt of court. The warrants for their arrest were to be issued on 16 June, and widespread strikes became imminent. However, as the result of a curious intervention by the Official Solicitor (an officer of the court), the Court of Appeal was able to review the decision to imprison, although the three dockers did not ask for it to be reviewed, and the decision was set aside. So the dockers did not go to prison and the strikes were avoided.[37]

For a fortnight there was a breathing space. Then on 3 July another complaint was lodged with the NIRC against seven dockers including two of the original three. On 7 July, the NIRC ordered them to refrain from their actions and, after further proceedings, on 21 July committed five of the seven to prison for contempt. Unofficial dock strikes began at once and the threat of widespread stoppages of work became very real.

On 24 July the General Secretary of the Trades Union Congress went to see the Prime Minister who said, according to *The Times*, that he would not intervene. On 25 July, the Official Solicitor visited the dockers in prison but they made clear that they did not intend to give any undertakings of obedience to the NIRC or to apologize – which is normally essential before those in contempt are released. Nevertheless the Official Solicitor on that day tried to persuade the NIRC to convene immediately so that he could apply for the committal orders to be discharged. But he was told to come back not later than the afternoon of the next day.

On 25 July the situation seemed to have reached an impasse. Sir John Donaldson, president of the NIRC, had said in June, 'By their conduct these men are saying they are above the rule of law. No court should ignore such a challenge. To do so would imperil all law and order.' On

71

21 July he said: 'These breaches are serious and were deliberately committed, quite literally in contempt of this court . . . The issue is whether these men are to be allowed to opt out of the rule of law . . . It is a very simple issue but vastly important for our whole way of life is based upon acceptance of the rule of law.' The NIRC had committed the men to prison. The men showed no intention of modifying their position. Dock strikes were occurring and a general strike was clearly impending. How could industrial action on a wide scale be avoided and the face of the NIRC be saved?

We have seen that on 13 June the Court of Appeal had decided in *Heaton's* case that the Transport and General Workers' Union was not accountable for the action of its shop stewards. From that decision, leave was given to appeal to the House of Lords. That appeal was heard between the 10th and 19th of July. Their Lordships reserved judgment and then, with almost unprecedented speed (at least eight weeks normally elapses), in a joint opinion given by Lord Wilberforce delivered their opinion, on the morning of 26 July – that 'next day' intimated to the Official Solicitor. And the House of Lords reversed the Court of Appeal and decided that the union was responsible for its shop stewards.[38] Immediately the NIRC convened and, avowedly because of that decision, released the dockers from prison.[39]

The difficulty is finding any necessary connection between two cases. The House of Lords' decision determined an important question of law concerning the liability of trade unions for the actions of their shop stewards. But the five dockers' case was about the 'very simple issue' of punishment for men who had defied the order of the NIRC and had expressed their intention to continue in that defiance. In releasing the dockers, the president of the NIRC said that, because of the House of Lords' decision, the situation was 'entirely changed'. The unions were accountable and the burden of their task would be 'immeasurably increased' if the dockers remained in prison.

'The cause of the rule of law will not be advanced by placing an avoidable burden upon the unions.' Nevertheless five men, who had been imprisoned because they deliberately and flagrantly disobeyed the orders of the NIRC, and so imperilled the rule of law and 'our whole way of life', were released although they had not asked to be released and had made clear that they had no intention of apologizing to the court for their behaviour or of desisting from that behaviour.

A political and economic crisis of possibly considerable dimensions was avoided by two actions. First, the speeding-up of the delivery of the House of Lords' decision; and secondly, the discovery by the NIRC that, because of that decision, they could release the dockers. It appeared very much as if the judicial system had bent itself to the needs of the politicians and that, in particular, the principles of the rule of law to which the NIRC earlier paid such respect had been sacrificed to the expediency of the political and economic situation.

This last example of judicial activism in political affairs differs from the others. The latter have shown a conservative judiciary interpreting legislation and developing the common law in ways which Government and Parliament sought to reverse. The establishment of the NIRC was a political act aimed at trying to contain trade union power within particular rules prescribed by the Industrial Relations Act 1971. The experiment failed and the NIRC was abolished in 1974. But the apparent willingness of the House of Lords to expedite the delivery of their judgment coupled with the highly eccentric use made of that judgment by the NIRC to release the five dockers was so convenient for the Government of the day that it aroused the strong suspicion of judicial compliance with political expediency.

A later industrial dispute was a pretty example of the intermingling of the exercise of powers in the high places of government in the United Kingdom. In October 1973, the NIRC fined the Amalgamated Union of Engineering

Workers £100,000 for contempt of court when they refused to obey the Court's order to call off a strike.[40]

To obtain payment of the fine the Court sequestrated against assets held in the political fund of the union. Labour MPs put down a motion in the House of Commons calling for the removal from office of the president of the Court for 'political prejudice and partiality'. Sir John Donaldson defended himself in a public speech saying that the Court had not known that the assets had been earmarked for a political or any other purpose. At this point Lord Hailsham, then Lord Chancellor, in a public speech and as head of the judiciary, attacked those who had signed the motion and said that the public should note the identity and party of the Members concerned. Whereupon Labour Members tabled another motion condemning the Lord Chancellor and alleging 'a gross contempt of the House of Commons'.[41]

In the event neither of the motions was debated and the matter lapsed.

The conflict between the courts and trade unions showed itself in the second half of the nineteenth century and the first decade of the twentieth as an expression of class conflict. The trade unions were growing in militancy, especially during the years after 1890, and were displaying powers which dismayed a large part of middle-class society. The dismay was in part because of the anticipated economic consequences of this militancy, but also because it threatened the existing social order of late Victorian England.

Many politicians, from Disraeli onwards, had realized that trade union power was an economic factor which had to be taken seriously into account and certainly was not capable of being overcome by crude shows of force. Her Majesty's judges, however, were less prescient and less capable of adjusting legal principles and traditions to the new pressures. So, under men like Halsbury, they reacted to the legislation of the later nineteenth century with all the inflexibility of those who are determined that what was good enough for their fathers' social and economic structures was good enough for them. And in the more general upheaval of political beliefs which accompanied 'the strange death of liberal England', influential judges were more often to be found towards the right of the spectrum of opinion.

The most recent developments may prove to be of the utmost importance and to have the most lasting consequences. What litigation might have been promoted by the Labour Government's aborted proposals in the late 1960s[42] we shall never know. But the much more rigorous policy embodied in the Conservatives' Industrial Relations Act of 1971 was a revolution in the long story. For this Act deliberately sought to use the courts and the judges to achieve political ends. The institution of the NIRC reflected the new techniques and re-introduced the old arguments. The identification of 'law' and 'policy' made almost impossible the continuance of the interplay between the judges and politicians which had provided a valuable tolerance. Had the Act succeeded, the damage to the reputation of judicial institutions would have been considerable; but it was always highly probable that this attempt to use the judges for these political purposes would fail. The failure was forecast by almost all those with the greatest knowledge of the working of industrial relations in this country and, more particularly, abroad. But the circumstances of its failure, and the manoeuvrings of politicians and judges which accompanied that failure, combined to produce a calamity which went far beyond the collapse of a doomed policy, for the failure directly resulted in a deep distrust of the judicial system. Trade unionists, as we have seen, had little cause to look to the judiciary for the protection of their statutory rights. Now the suspected subservience of the judiciary to the politicians seemed to be made manifest. There is no evidence that the judges at any time protested to Her Majesty's Government in or out of Parliament against the proposals to involve them directly and indirectly in the administration of the Act of 1971. Their failure to do so rests with the Lord Chancellor (Lord Hailsham), the Master of the Rolls (Lord Denning), and, to a lesser extent, the Lord Chief Justice (Lord Widgery).

The events of 1972 finally persuaded the leaders of organized labour (and the great mass of trade union members) that the judges were not to be trusted. Today the relations between the trade unions and the judiciary are worse than they were in the period immediately following the *Taff Vale* decision in 1901. Mr Heath deliberately employed the judges as instruments of his policy, enmeshed trade unionists in new legal rules, and then, in chorus with the judges, condemned them, in the name of the rule of law, for seeking to extricate themselves.

Less easy to understand is the apparent willingness of the judiciary to lend themselves to this manoeuvring. It is difficult to believe in the political naïveté of judges, but Sir John Donaldson, president of the NIRC, looking back on the short history of that court, has expressed views which are bewildering in their ingenuousness. He emphasized the need for guidelines in all aspects of industrial relations and continued:

With such guidelines, the courts could be given their traditional role of investigating the merits of disputes and helping the party who is right . . . The public suffers from every industrial dispute. Ought they not to know who is right? Adopting this new approach they *would* know, for the court which investigated the dispute would tell them. Those who suffered injustice would then be supported by the courts.[43]

On this evidence it seems possible that a large part of the conflict that arose in the administration of the NIRC was the result of a belief of its president that, in industrial conflicts, one side can be discovered, after proper examination by judges, to be 'right' and the other side 'wrong'. But industrial conflicts are not of this kind. They can be solved only by compromise and by the exercise of economic and political strength, not by the application of legal principles or guidelines. This may be unfortunate but it is the reason why the NIRC was bound to fail.

NOTES

1. See generally K. W. Wedderburn, *The Worker and the Law* (2nd ed. 1971) on which I have drawn heavily for much of what follows.

2. John Saville, 'Trade Unions and Free Labour: The background to the Taff Vale Decision' in *Essays in Labour History* (ed. Asa Briggs and John Saville, 1960) Vol. 1, p. 317.

3. Including *Lyons v. Wilkins* (see below pp. 65-6).

4. [1898] A. C. 1.

5. Here and elsewhere this means the House in its judicial capacity.

6. R. F. V. Heuston, *Lives of the Lord Chancellors 1885-1940*, pp. 119-20.

7. [1901] A. C. 495.

8. *Mogul Steamship Co. v. McGregor Gow & Co.* [1892] A. C. 25.

9. *Taff Vale Railway Co. v. Amalgamated Society of Railway Servants* [1901] A. C. 426.

10. Heuston, *op cit*, p. 76; G. M. Young, *Stanley Baldwin*, p. 31.

11. G. M. Young, *ibid*.

12. *Ibid.*, p. 32.

13. Quoted by Wedderburn, *op cit*, p. 317.

14. *Amalgamated Society of Railway Servants v. Osborne* [1910] A. C. 87.

15. See S and B Webb, *The History of Trade Unionism*, pp. 608-26.

16. 195 H. C. Deb. col. 584-6.

17. *Ibid.* col. 787.

18. *Ibid.* col. 862-4.

19. Was this perhaps what Astbury J. was going to say?

20. *National Sailors and Firemen's Union of Great Britain v. Reed* (1926) Ch. 536.

21. For a powerful argument that Astbury J. was wrong in law, see A. L. Goodhart in 36 Yale Law Journal (1926-27) p. 464.

22. [1896] 1 Ch. 811; [1899] 1 Ch. 255.

23. *Piddington v. Bates* [1960] 3 All. E. R. 660.

24. [1967] 1 Q.B. 91.

25. *Hunt v. Broome* [1974] A. C. 587.

26. *Kavanagh v. Hiscock* [1974] 2 W. L. R. 421; see also *Hubbard v. Pitt* [1975] 3 W. L. R. 201 (see below pp. 145-6).

27. For the *Shrewsbury* case, see below p. 136.

28. Mr John Mortimer, QC.

29. [1964] A. C. 1129.

30. *Thomson & Co. v. Deakin* [1952] 1 Ch. 646.

31. *Stratford v. Lindley* [1965] A. C. 269.

32. [1969] 2 Ch. 106.

33. Wedderburn *op cit*, p. 336.

34. Quoted by Wedderburn *op cit*, p. 8.

35. *Heaton's Transport (St Helens) Ltd v. T.G.W.U.* [1972] 1 I. C. R. 285.

36. *Ibid.* 308; [1973] A. C. 15.

37. *The Times* June 12 and 14, 1972.

38. [1972] 1 I. C. R. 308; 1973 A. C. 15. Subsequently however it appeared that this was not a proposition of general application: see *General Aviation Services v. T.G.W.U.* [1976] I. R. L. R. 224 a decision which seemed to indicate a desire by the House of Lords (Lord Salmon dissenting) to put the decision in *Heaton's* case behind them.

39. *The Times* 27 July 1972.

40. *Con-Mech (Engineers) Ltd v. A.U.E.W.* [1973] I. C. R. 620.

41. See 865 H. C. Deb. col. 1089-91, 1291-7.

42. See *In Place of Strife* (Cmnd 3888).

43. *Lessons from the Industrial Court* (1975) 91 L. Q. R. at 191-2.

Chapter 4: Personal rights

INDIVIDUAL FREEDOM

Traditionally judges are thought of as the defenders of the rights of individuals from attack by public authorities. In recent years this tradition has been upheld only spasmodically.

In 1939 the Government took powers by Defence Regulations to detain persons without trial but these powers were expressed in those Regulations to be exercisable only 'if the Secretary of State has reasonable cause to believe' that a person had hostile associations. The use of the limiting adjective, one would have thought, clearly empowered the courts to review the reasonableness of the 'cause'. But the House of Lords in *Liversidge v. Anderson*[1] held otherwise. This was a considerable abdication by the courts, in circumstances of national emergency, of their controlling jurisdiction.

Yet this decision was also a rallying ground for those who believed that, especially where a man's personal freedom was involved, the powers of the executive should be strictly interpreted. For this was the case in which Lord Atkin, alone against such powerful colleagues as Lords Maugham, MacMillan, Wright and Romer, delivered the most highly influential minority opinion in the English courts of the twentieth century. In the course of his judgment he said:

I view with apprehension the attitude of judges who on a mere question of construction when face to face with claims involving the liberty of the subject show themselves more executive minded than the executive. Their function is to give words their natural meaning, not, perhaps, in wartime leaning towards liberty, but following the dictum of Pollock C.B. in *Bowditch v. Balchin*[2] cited with approval by my noble and learned friend Lord Wright in *Barnard v. Gorman*[3]: 'In a case in which the liberty of the subject is concerned, we cannot go beyond the natural construction of the statute.' In this country, amid the clash of arms, the laws are not silent. They may be changed, but they speak the same language in war as in peace. It has always been one of the pillars of freedom, one of the principles of liberty for which on recent authority we are now fighting, that the judges are no respecters of persons and stand between the subject and any attempted encroachments on his liberty by the executive, alert to see that any coercive action is justified in law. In this case I have listened to arguments which might have been addressed acceptably to the Court of King's Bench in the time of Charles I.

Liversidge v. Anderson was a wartime case and the powers of detention without trial (internment) were conferred on the Executive under an express statutory provision which authorized the making of regulations 'for the detention of persons whose detention appears to the Secretary of State to be expedient in the interests of public safety or the defence of the realm'.[4] The comparable legislation passed for the purposes of the 1914-18 war contained no express powers authorizing internment but in *R. v Halliday*[5] the majority in the House of Lords held that general words in the Defence of the Realm Act 1914 were sufficient, a view from which Lord Shaw dissented. In contrast, it was later held by Mr Justice Salter that a similar exercise of powers, this time to take property without payment of full compensation, was illegal.[6] Here, as elsewhere, the courts seemed to be more concerned to protect property rights than rights of personal freedom. In *R. v. Governor of Wormwood Scrubs Prison*[7] it was held by the Divisional Court that the internment powers extended to cover the situation in Ireland even after the war was over.

The decision of the majority in *Liversidge v. Anderson* effectively meant that the Minister's order authorizing internment could not be questioned because the Minister could not be required to show on what basis his order had been made. The general principle that this is the proper interpretation of the words 'If the Minister has reasonable cause to believe' has been doubted[8] and two recent decisions in Northern Ireland courts have suggested that improper arrest or a failure to provide the internee with a statement of the material on which the internment was based is sufficient for the internment order to be set aside.[9]

However the majority decisions in *R. v. Halliday* and *Liversidge v. Anderson* were referred to with approval by Lord Denning in *R. v. Secretary of State ex parte Hosenball* in 1977 (*The Times*, 30 March 1977) where an American journalist lost his appeal against deportation under the Immigration Act 1971. The decision to deport was challenged in the Court of Appeal on the ground that there had been a breach of the rules of natural justice in that the Home Secretary had refused to tell the appellant any of the details on the basis of which the Home Secretary had decided that the appellant was a security risk.

In a remarkable passage Lord Denning MR seemed to accept that the courts had no part to play because the Government never erred. *The Times* reported him thus:

His Lordship's conclusion was that there was a conflict between the interests of national security and the freedom of the individual. The balance between the two was not for a court of law but for the Home Secretary. He was the person entrusted by our constitution with the task. In some parts of the world security had on occasion been used as an excuse for all sorts of infringements of individual liberty. But not in England. Because during the war and after successive ministers had discharged their duties to the complete satisfaction of the people at large. They had set up tribunals, often with a legal chairman, to ensure that justice was done. They had never interfered with the liberty or the freedom of movement of any individual except where it was absolutely necessary for the safety of the state.

It is well known that unlawful detention may be challenged by means of an application for habeas corpus but the courts sometimes withhold that remedy for political reasons.

Dr Sharpe summarizes his extensive examination of the authorities on habeas corpus and other remedies thus:

This review of the authorities demonstrates that habeas corpus can be an effective remedy to control the exercise of discretionary power, but that policy considerations may often make the courts reluctant to act. There are several habeas corpus cases which illustrate the ordinary rule of the reviewability of executive action and, most recently, the law of immigration has provided examples. On the other hand it is submitted that the cases which involve emergency powers indicate a reluctance on the part of the courts to use the remedy of habeas corpus to its full potential. Judicial innovation would not have been required to justify intervention in *Halliday* or in *Greene* and *Liversidge v. Anderson*. In each case, accepted principles of constitutional and administrative law were available and applicable. In *Halliday*, and almost certainly in *Greene* and in *Liversidge v. Anderson*, the legal arguments weighed against the result reached, and the judges acted on policy grounds.[10]

When it is remembered that habeas corpus is not a discretionary remedy, this amounts to saying that the judiciary, despite all the rhetoric which they pour out in praise of this ancient writ, are willing to deny it to an imprisoned applicant, who in law should be set free, because they consider that the politics of the situation entitle them to do so. This is not what is generally understood to be the function of the courts.

POLICE POWERS

Police powers and their exercise frequently result in the judiciary drawing and redrawing the lines of what they consider to be permissible and impermissible conduct. In a leading case from the 1930s, a public meeting was held to protest against the Incitement to Disaffection Bill then before Parliament and to demand the dismissal of the chief constable of Glamorgan. Between 500 and 700 people were present. James Sawkins, a sergeant of the Glamorgan County Police, sought admission to the meeting, was told at the door that police officers were not to be admitted, but nevertheless (with other policemen) entered and sat in the front row. At one point Alun Thomas 'laid a hand' on one of the policemen (an inspector) and Sergeant Sawkins pushed his hand away saying 'I won't allow you to interfere with my superior officer'. Neither Alun Thomas nor Sergeant Sawkins used more force than was reasonably necessary to effect their purposes. Alun Thomas charged Sergeant Sawkins with unlawful assault. The Divisional Court held that a police officer was entitled, as part of his duty of preventing crime, to enter private premises when he had reasonable ground for believing that an offence was imminent or likely to be committed and that Sergeant Sawkins was properly acquitted.[11]

At the end of May 1933, Katherine Duncan of the National Unemployed Workers' Movement addressed a street meeting following which 'a disturbance took place'. On 30 July 1934 she again began to address a meeting at the same place, although told by a police inspector that she could not, whereupon she was arrested and taken into custody. It was not alleged that she or any of the persons present at the meeting had either committed, incited or provoked any breach of the peace. The Divisional Court held that she had been properly convicted of wilfully obstructing the police who 'reasonably apprehended a breach of the peace'.[12]

The difficulty and danger of such decisions is that so much discretion resides in the police and neither the courts nor the legislature are willing to lay down any guidelines. This gives rise to suspicion that the police will prosecute one person advocating one set of views while not prosecuting another advocating a different set of views. Certainly this was the impression conveyed when Pat Arrowsmith was convicted of obstructing the highway when addressing a meeting at a place where such meetings were frequently held and where previously no prosecutions had followed. 'That,' said the Lord Chief Justice, speaking without apparent irony, 'of course, has nothing to do with this court. The sole question here is whether the defendant has contravened section 121(1) of the Highways Act 1959.'[13]

The laws relating to arrest, to questioning, to accessibility to lawyers, to search and to seizure of goods, come frequently before the courts for elucidation. And the judges are immediately faced with the constantly recurring dilemma posed by the impossibility of being, at one and the same time, the protectors of personal rights and key performers in the preservation of law and order.

For many years a statement of principles called the Judges' Rules – because made by them – has been made public. These are not rules of law but indicate what the judges consider to be proper practice. They provide for the 'cautions' which the police should put before a person makes a statement to the police, indicating that he is not obliged to say anything but that, if he does so, it will be taken down in writing and may be used in evidence. If a person at his trial gives an account of what took place which he did not give to the police when cautioned, the judge is not permitted to suggest to the jury that this account is false because, if it had been true, he would have told the police. In 1964, the Criminal Law Revision

Committee was asked by the Home Secretary to consider these matters and in 1972 they reported. Amongst other things, they proposed that this 'right of silence' should be removed in the sense that the inference of falsity could be drawn to the attention of the jury.

In these matters of evidence and proof, the judiciary have a variable record. Recently a defendant who refused to answer police questions was held not to have obstructed the police.[14] On the other hand where a confession was obtained without the usual caution having been given, the Court of Appeal held in 1971 that the confession was admissible if the judge decided that it was made voluntarily.[15] And an interrogation in a police station need not, it has been held, be preceded by cautions (even when the person questioned has been arrested) if at the time of the interrogation the police have no information which could be put before the court as the beginnings of a case.[16]

Nevertheless, the reaction of some members of the judiciary to the proposals of the Criminal Law Revision Committee was strongly adverse and did much to (at least) postpone the implementation of the recommendations, as did a similar reaction from members of the legal profession.[17]

It may be of the utmost importance to know whether an arrest is being made. An arrested man who runs away commits an offence; and a charge of unlawful arrest will fail if there was no arrest. So also, a blood specimen may be taken to support a charge of driving while drunk only if the driver has been arrested. If a police constable says, 'I shall have to ask you to come to the police station for further tests', is that a request or an order? Only if it is, in the circumstances, an order, will the words imply an arrest. Local justices in such a case decided it was not an arrest and the higher court refused to disagree with them, the question being so much one of fact.[18]

Elias v. Pasmore[19] is a leading case on search and seizure. The plaintiffs were the lessees of the headquarters of the National Unemployed Workers' Movement. Walter

Hannington (one of the plaintiffs) made a speech in Trafalgar Square in consequence of which a warrant for his arrest was issued. The defendant police inspectors entered the headquarters, arrested Hannington, and seized a number of documents, some of which were used at the trial of the plaintiff Elias on a charge of inciting Hannington to commit the crime of sedition. The plaintiffs claimed the return of those documents, and the question was whether their seizure was lawful, since they had no relevance to the charge against Hannington and no search warrant had or would have been obtained. The court decided that, though the original seizure of the documents was 'improper', it was 'justified' because they were capable of being used, and were used, as evidence in the trial of Elias.

In 1969 police officers enquiring into the disappearance of a woman they believed to have been murdered, searched (without a warrant) the house of her father-in-law. At their request he handed them the passports of himself, his wife and daughter. Subsequently these persons, being Pakistanis and wishing to visit Pakistan, asked for the return of the passports but the police refused. The court ordered their return but in the course of his judgment Lord Denning, summarizing the law where police officers enter a man's home without a warrant, said:

> I take it to be settled law . . . that the officers are entitled to take any goods which they find in his possession or in his house which they reasonably believe to be material evidence in relation to the crime . . . for which they enter. If in the course of their search they come upon any other goods which show him to be implicated in some other crime, they may take them provided they act reasonably and detain them no longer than is necessary.[20]

Two years later in another case, police officers, armed with a warrant authorizing them to enter premises to search for explosives, found none but seized a large number of leaflets and posters, contending that these were evidence of a crime such as conspiracy to pervert the course of justice or to commit contempt of court. The police claimed further that they needed to retain the documents for comparison with other documents purporting to emanate from a criminal organization responsible for causing explosions. The court held that the police were entitled to seize the documents and that they had established they were acting reasonably and were detaining the documents no longer than necessary.[21]

The general trend of these cases is alarming. It comes very close to giving the police a right to search and to seize douments which have nothing to do either with the warrant (if they have one) or with the original purpose of their investigations. It is an old tradition that general warrants to arrest unspecified persons and to search property at large are illegal and are not justifiable on the ground of the public interest. The tradition is beginning to look less strong than it did. The danger of placing so sharp a weapon in the hands of the Government and of the police is very obvious.

RACE RELATIONS

In 1965 the Race Relations Act was passed making discrimination on the ground of colour, race, ethnic or national origins unlawful in certain circumstances. These provisions were expanded by the Race Relations Act 1968. In 1972 came the first of a series of leading cases.

Stanislaw Zesko was born and bred a Polish national and joined the Polish Air Force. In November 1939, after the Nazi invasion of Poland, he escaped to France, came to the United Kingdom, enlisted in the Royal Air Force, and completed three operational tours in Bomber Command. After the war he remained in the United Kingdom, married and for fourteen years lived in the borough of Ealing in conditions of great hardship. He was, said the judge who first heard the case, 'a man of perfect character and integrity and a wholly admirable person'. In 1966, and again in 1968, Mr Zesko applied to be placed on the housing waiting list of Ealing Borough Council. His applications were refused under a council rule that an applicant had to be 'a British subject within the meaning of the British Nationality Act 1948'. A complaint was made to the Race Relations Board which, after investigation, notified the council that its action was one of unlawful discrimination because the Race Relations Act 1968 made unlawful the special treatment of a person on the ground of his national origins. The council applied to the courts for a declaration that its rule was not unlawful. The House of Lords, by a majority of four to one, decided in favour of the council on the ground that 'national origins' did not mean 'nationality' which was what the council's rule was concerned with.[22]

The approach of the majority was linguistic and formalistic.[23] Viscount Dilhorne argued that Parliament could have used the word 'nationality' and the failure to do so indicated that discrimination on the ground of nationality was meant to be excluded from the Act. It was also argued that to interpret national origins so as to include nationality would extend its meaning in a different context and enlarge the scope of the criminal offence of stirring up hatred under the Act of 1965.

More serious because affecting more people were two decisions about clubs which the House of Lords decided in 1973 and 1974.

In April 1969 Mr Amarjit Singh Shah who was employed in the Post Office and was a Conservative (having joined the local association in 1966) applied to join the East Ham South Conservative Club. He was proposed and seconded. When his application was considered by the committee, the chairman indicated in reply to a question that he regarded the colour of Mr Shah's skin as relevant and, on the chairman's casting vote, Mr Shah's application for membership was rejected. Mr Shah complained to the

Race Relations Board, who issued a plaint against the club. The county court judge rejected the plaint, the Court of Appeal upheld it, and the House of Lords by a majority of four to one rejected it.[24] The Race Relations Act of 1968 provides that it is unlawful for any person concerned with the provision to the public or a section of the public of any services, etc., to discriminate. The majority decided that the Club members were not 'a section of the public'.

In the second case[25] a member of a dockers' club in Preston took in as his guest Mr Sherrington, a coloured man. Mr Sherrington was told by the secretary to leave ('We do not serve coloured people'). Mr Sherrington was a member of another club in Preston which had no colour bar. Both these clubs, and some 4000 others, were banded together in a union and each member of one club was an associate member of all others in the union. The question was whether associates were 'a section of the public'. The county court judge and the Court of Appeal found for the Race Relations Board. But the House of Lords unanimously found for the Club.

How did it come about that the judges who sat in the Court of Appeal and the House of Lords in these two cases differed so markedly? The answer seems to be that they took one of two different 'political' views.

The conservative view is that Parliament should intervene as little as possible in matters about which people differ in large numbers and that statutes should be so interpreted. No doubt motives are mixed when intervention to control racial discrimination is discouraged. But Lord Diplock in the *Dockers' Club* case put it thus, referring to the Race Relations Act:

This is a statute which, however admirable its motives, restricts the liberty which the citizen has previously enjoyed at common law to differentiate between one person and another in entering or declining to enter into transactions with them . . . The arrival in this country within recent years of many immigrants from disparate and distant lands has brought a new dimension to the problem of the legal right to discriminate against the stranger. If everyone were rational and humane – or, for that matter, Christian – no legal sanctions would be needed to prevent one man being treated by his fellow men less favourably than another *simply upon the ground of his colour, race or ethnic or national origins.* But in the field of domestic or social intercourse differentiation in treatment of individuals is unavoidable . . . Thus, in discouraging the intrusion of coercion by legal process in the fields of domestic or social intercourse, the principle of effectiveness joins force with the broader principle of freedom to order one's private life as one chooses. [Italics in the original.]

This view begins with the private rights of the individual, including the right to discriminate on the ground of the colour of a man's skin. In interpreting an Act of Parliament, it assumes that those rights are to be diminished to the extent necessary to make sense of the legislation but no further. Therefore within the spectrum of happenings which range from the way a family makes provision for its friends within the home to the conduct of an open market, the definition of 'a section of the public' must be restricted as tightly as possible.

The alternative view does not found itself on this individualist position, does not think primarily of private rights. It makes other assumptions. It seeks to interpret the Race Relations Act in a way which will extend its operation and not restrict it, while recognizing that the Act clearly means to avoid intervention in the domestic sphere and in other private gatherings (certainly including some clubs). It regards racial discrimination not as an individual right but as a social wrong.[26]

One of the most remarkable decisions of the Court of Appeal since 1965 was in *R. v. Race Relations Board ex parte Selvarajan.*[27] The applicant, a graduate of Madras and London Universities, was appointed in 1961 to the

City of Westminster (now Walbrook) College as a lecturer grade 1. Most lecturers are promoted to grade 2 within a few years. S was never promoted during fourteen years. He felt this was because of his colour or race and he complained to the Race Relations Board. The case was referred to a conciliation committee under the Race Relations Act 1968. A subcommittee ('a group of able men and women, holding positions of responsibility') investigated. The secretary of the committee met the principal of the college and other members of staff, the applicant, and representatives of the Inner London Education Authority (the employers). She then reported to the subcommittee. Between May 1971 and February 1972 the subcommittee received representations in writing and orally from all concerned. They gave each side a full opportunity of meeting everything that was said on the other side. They discussed the case at length between themselves. 'It must,' said Lord Denning, 'have taken many hours.' The subcommittee agreed to recommend that unlawful discrimination had taken place. The full conciliation committee met and came to the same opinion. In March 1972, after attempts at conciliation, the education officer of ILEA rejected the opinion and required the matter to be further investigated by the Race Relations Board.

The Race Relations Board referred the matter to their employment committee of seven members to each of whom was sent a file containing a record (over 100 pages) of the proceedings before the conciliation committee. In June 1972 the employment committee met and decided to reinvestigate the matter themselves. The reinvestigation was made in this way. In August 1972 Mrs C, a conciliation officer, wrote to the ILEA with a summary of the applicant's complaint. On 17 November 1972 they replied in detail and attached a statement which covered sixteen pages. On 24 November, Mrs C wrote to the applicant setting out several points which might be regarded as adversely affecting his case, and asking him to tell her by 8 December whether he wished to reply in writing or to appear personally. The applicant did not reply by that date nor before 13 December when the employment committee met. Meanwhile on 4 December 1972 Mrs C prepared a report for the Board headed 'Clearly Predictable Case – Full papers to Mota Singh' (who was a member of the employment committee and a barrister). There followed a short summary of the complaint and the answer in one-and-a-half pages and a recommendation 'That the committee form an opinion of no unlawful discrimination.'

At the meeting of the employment committee on 13 December, Mota Singh sent his apologies for inability to attend and said he agreed with the recommendation. Four of the six members of the committee present had not had all the papers. The chairman said he agreed with Mota Singh and the other members agreed. On 10 January 1973 the employment committee reconsidered the matter with Mota Singh present and confirmed its previous opinion.

In all this story the matter which most troubled the Court of Appeal was that four members of the employment committee were not in a position to form an opinion of their own because they were not in possession of all the information. But, said Lord Denning, of the employment committee of seven members, 'It is impossible to suppose that all of them need sit to determine a matter, or that all of those who sit should have read all the papers or heard all the evidence . . . In my opinion the applicant's complaint had been fully investigated in accordance with the statute. He has been most fairly treated. And the Race Relations Board formed an opinion which was manifestly correct, that there had been no unlawful discrimination against him.' The applicant's case was dismissed.

The members of the Court of Appeal were clearly most reluctant to interfere with the decision of the Race Relations Board. And, no doubt, this reluctance is often justifiable. But in this case the disparities between the ways in which the conciliation committee and the employment committee proceeded were so glaring that the propriety of the employment committee's actions was surely in question. The conciliation subcommittee had seen all the parties and had investigated the matter at great length. The employment committee saw none of those concerned, were presented with a prejudicial recommendation by an officer who had seen none of those concerned, and came to a conclusion although four of its seven members had not seen all the papers. How in the light of all this could Lord Denning conclude that the opinion of the Race Relations Board was 'manifestly correct'? How could he conclude that the applicant had been 'most fairly treated'?

IMMIGRATION AND DEPORTATION

Before 1962 a Commonwealth citizen was entitled to enter the United Kingdom, but the Commonwealth Immigrants Act of that year empowered an immigration officer to refuse admission or to admit only on conditions (including limitation of length of stay). That power was not to be exercised if the applicant satisfied the immigration officer that he or she was ordinarily resident in the United Kingdom and had been so resident at any time within the previous two years, or was the wife, or child under 16, of a resident. The power of immigration officers to examine any intending immigrant lapsed 24 hours after the immigrant landed.

In *Re H.K.*[28] where the age of a child, said to be under 16, was doubted by an immigration officer, the Divisional Court refused an application for habeas corpus and upheld the officer's refusal to admit. The Court said they could review the decision if it had been come to 'unfairly', but that that was not so in this case. This indicated that the Court took a limited view of its functions. In *Re A.*[29] the doubt was whether the child was the plaintiff's son and the Court of Appeal refused to interfere so long as the immigration officers acted 'honestly and fairly'. However, in *Ex parte Amrik Singh*[30] where the immigration officer refused permission because he suspected that the applicant was not a genuine visitor for a short period (as he claimed to be), the Divisional Court sent the matter back to the immigration authorities to be reconsidered.

In *Ex parte Ahsan*[31] eleven Pakistanis landed clandestinely (but not illegally) and were arrested shortly afterwards; the question was whether, in an application for habeas corpus, the onus lay on them to prove that their landing had taken place more than 24 hours earlier or on the authorities to prove it had taken place within that period. The Divisional Court held that it was the latter and ordered the release of those arrested. But in *Re Wazid Hassan*[32] the Divisional Court held that, in an application for habeas corpus, it was for the detained person to show that his detention as an illegal immigrant was unlawful.

The most important of these cases under the Act of 1962 was *D.P.P. v. Bhagwan*[33]. Here again the immigrant landed clandestinely. Some two years later he was arrested and charged with conspiring to evade the control on immigration imposed by the Act of 1962. It was argued on his behalf that, as he had not acted illegally by landing as he did, the charge disclosed no offence known to the law. This gave rise to discussion about the limits of conspiracy and of *Shaw*'s case[34]. The House of Lords gave judgment, unanimously, for the immigrant.

The practical importance of this decision for immigrants was much reduced by the Commonwealth Immigrants Act 1968, which made clandestine landings an offence, and the law was further tightened by the Immigration Act 1971, which declared an 'illegal entrant' to be anyone who had entered the United Kingdom in breach of the immigration laws. In this sense the Act of 1971 was retroactive[35]. But in *R. v. Miah*[36], the House of Lords refused to apply penal provisions of that Act retroactively so as to render a person liable to criminal proceedings for acts which were not criminal when he committed them.

Since 1969, there has been a right of appeal in some circumstances from the decision of an immigration officer to an adjudicator and to an Immigration Appeal Tribunal. Even so, the courts will intervene if they consider that the adjudicator, or the Tribunal, has made an error in law or has acted in breach of the rules of natural justice. Probably in these immigration cases the courts would be reluctant to overrule the appellate authorities, but where a student, who had entered the United Kingdom on a 12-month study permit, was first refused an extension and then subsequently, after various errors in the Home Office, refused leave to appeal, the Court of Appeal overruled the Tribunal and allowed her to stay.[37] Similarly, when the Home Office tried to insist that an immigrant, who claimed she had an unrestricted right to enter the United Kingdom, must apply for the necessary certificate in India and not in the United Kingdom, the Court of Appeal upheld her right to make application in the United Kingdom.[38]

Section 14 of the Immigration Act 1971 gives a right of appeal to an immigrant who has a limited leave to remain in the United Kingdom but is refused an extension by the Secretary of State. In *Ex parte Subramanian*,[39] the Court of Appeal held that the application for an extension must be made before and not after the limited leave has expired. If this were done the applicant might stay until the appeal was decided. But in *Suthendran v. Immigration Appeal Tribunal*[40] the House of Lords by a majority held that if an immigrant applies for an extension before his limited leave has expired but the Secretary of State does not give his decision until after the date of expiration, then the immigrant can no longer appeal because he no longer 'has' a limited leave to remain. This absurdly pedantic and literal interpretation means that the immigrant may be deprived of his right to appeal by the Secretary of State deliberately or carelessly failing to decide before the date of expiration.[41]

With those cases may be contrasted two concerning other applicants for admission. Robert Soblen, a citizen of the USA, was convicted of conspiracy to obtain and hand over information valuable to the Soviet Union. While on bail he fled to Israel whence he was removed and put on a flight, in the custody of a United States marshal, which was due to stop at London en route for New York. About 20 minutes out of London he inflicted severe wounds on himself with a knife and on arrival at London was put in an ambulance and taken to hospital. From there, having been refused political asylum, he applied for a writ of habeas corpus claiming that he was being wrongly detained. Everything turned on whether he had been given leave to land. Attempts had been made when his aircraft landed to serve him with a notice refusing him leave but he was too ill to receive it. Nevertheless the Court of Appeal held that he had been refused leave. In the lower court, the Lord Chief Justice said that he was in no way concerned with whether or not Soblen was, as he contended, innocent of the charges of which he had been convicted and this view was repeated in the Court of Appeal.[42] But the suspicion remained that the deportation order would not have been upheld but for the diplomatic relations between the countries concerned. Shortly before he was due to be flown out of the United Kingdom *en route* for New York, Soblen took an overdose of drugs and died.

Aliens are normally allowed to enter the country if they come 'for the purpose of full-time study at a recognized educational establishment' and until 25 July 1968 the Hubbard College of Scientology was so recognized. On that date the Minister of Health told the House of Commons that scientology was 'so objectionable that it would be right to take all steps . . . to curb its growth', and that 'foreign nationals already in the United Kingdom for study at a Scientology establishment' would not be granted extension of stay. The plaintiffs were refused leave to extend their stay and brought an action claiming that the Home Secretary was bound to consider their applications on their merits and not merely follow the general statement of policy. By a majority the Court of Appeal dismissed their action. Lord Denning put strong emphasis on the power of the Home Secretary to refuse to admit any alien, without giving any reason. All that was necessary was that the exclusion was for 'an authorized purpose'. He said:

> I think the Minister can exercise his power for any purpose which he considers to be for the public good or to be in the interests of the people of this country.[43]

In effect, in this and other cases, the courts refuse to review the exercise of the Minister's discretion. As they express the principle, it is virtually impossible for a plaintiff to show that the Minister has acted for an unauthorized purpose.

CONTEMPT OF COURT, RESTRICTIONS ON PUBLICATIONS, AND THE MAINTENANCE OF SECRECY

A recent report stated that the law relating to contempt of court had developed over the centuries as a means whereby the courts might act to prevent or punish conduct which tended to obstruct, prejudice or abuse the administration of justice.[44] Such conduct may take place, in relation to any particular case, before, during or after the trial. Most obviously, if the court makes an order which is disregarded, that is contempt, as happened when trade unions were fined for failing to obey orders of the National Industrial Relations Court; or as happens in matrimonial cases where parties disobey orders not to molest or invade the privacy of other parties.

But, less usually, there may be positive disruption as when, in 1970, a group of Welsh students invaded a court in the Royal Courts of Justice in London and broke up the hearing of a case by striding into the well of the court, shouting slogans, scattering pamphlets and singing. They did this to demonstrate for the preservation of the Welsh language, and those who refused to apologize to the judge were instantly committed by him to three months' imprisonment. On appeal they were bound over for 12 months to be of good behaviour. The members of the

Court of Appeal emphasized that the right to protest must be executed within the law. But their judgments also established, despite statutory law which seemed, as applicable to these students, to require that their sentences should be suspended, that the High Court still had power at common law to commit instantly to prison for such contempt.[45]

Clearly the position of an accused person may be adversely and unfairly affected if, before his trial is concluded, publicity about him appears in the press. This may well create prejudice, not least in the mind of any member of the jury. So for a newspaper to describe an accused person of having had an unedifying career as brothel-keeper, procurer and property racketeer is a serious contempt of court – and when this happened in 1967 the *Sunday Times* was fined £5,000.[46]

In an earlier case, two journalists who gave evidence to a tribunal of enquiry investigating breaches of security by an Admiralty clerk refused to disclose the sources of information which they had published. This tribunal was by statute in a similar position, in relation to contempt, as the High Court, and the Court of Appeal upheld sentences of six and three months' imprisonment.[47]

These and other cases are now overshadowed by the decision of the House of Lords in the 'thalidomide' case.[48] The story is long and complicated but, put very briefly, between 1959 and 1961 a company made and marketed under licence a drug containing thalidomide, as a result of which about 450 children were born with gross deformities. In 1968 and subsequently actions were begun by the issue of writs against the company and some of these were settled out of court. For others, negotiations continued and in September 1972 the *Sunday Times* published the first of a series of articles to draw attention to the plight of the children. The company complained to the Attorney-General that the article was a contempt of court because some actions were still pending. The editor justified the article and at the same time sent to the

Attorney and to the company for comment a second article in draft (for which he claimed complete factual accuracy) on the testing, manufacture and marketing of the drug. The Attorney-General asked the courts to grant an injunction to prevent the publication of this second article on the ground that it was a contempt. The Divisional Court granted the injunction but the Court of Appeal refused it. The House of Lords allowed the company's appeal and granted the injunction.

Essentially, the view of the Court of Appeal[49] was that in the unique circumstances of a national tragedy where the public interest required that the issues should be discussed, where the legal proceedings had been dormant for years, and where there appeared no possibility of any action coming to trial, the law of contempt which restrained comment did not apply. The public interest in fair comment outweighed the possible prejudice to a party. The House of Lords decided against the *Sunday Times* because the articles were 'intended to bring pressure to bear' on the company. The enormous pressure which the company brought to bear on the parents of the children to accept the settlement first offered (which was very small compared with the amount offered after the public campaign in the press, Parliament and elsewhere) was presumably not considered relevant. The public interest in proper discussion in the circumstances of this case and the weakness of the parents' situation unless they could be championed by the press appeared to carry very little weight with their Lordships whose decision was unnecessary in law and deplorable in practice.

The power of the court to prevent publication was further shown in *R. v. Socialist Worker*[50] when during a trial for blackmail the judge directed that the two victims should be referred to as Mr Y and Mr Z. A journalist published their names and he and the publishers were held guilty of contempt and each was fined £250. No doubt there are cases (particularly involving children) when names should be withheld from publication. But the present law is unclear and drawn with so broad a brush that there can be no certainty that secrecy is imposed in only the small number of necessary instances. So also the present law operates so uncertainly that editors and journalists are forced to withhold comment on matters greatly affecting the public interest long before there can be any question of possibly influencing or prejudicing any trial. And although individual judges have criticized the existing laws, others have interpreted them in ways which have extended rather than diminished their scope. So public comment has been stifled.[51] And even the House of Commons has adopted a highly restrictive rule of procedure limiting the discussion of matters *sub judice.*[52]

Quite apart from the provisions of the Official Secrets Acts, political restrictions have been imposed on former Ministers on the extent to which they reveal what took place when they were in Government. This applies most strongly to former Cabinet Ministers who have normally been required to submit to the Secretary to the Cabinet drafts of their proposed publications. Mr R. H. S. Crossman kept a diary during the six years from 1964 to 1970 when he was a member of the Cabinet. Thereafter he began to collate his records and had completed and handed to his publishers the first volume before his death in April 1974. On 10 May 1974, one of the publishers, who was also a literary executor of Mr Crossman, sent a copy of the typescript of this volume (which dealt with the period 1964-6) to the Cabinet Secretary asking for 'a reasonably quick reading' as publication was planned for that autumn. On 22 June the Secretary said that he could not agree to publication of this volume. He said there were two complementary principles. The first was the collective responsibility of the Cabinet and the need to maintain secrecy to ensure completely frank discussion within the Cabinet and its committees. The second was the personal responsibility of individual Ministers. Further correspondence followed and the *Sunday Times* published some extracts from the diaries not all of which had been 'cleared' by the Cabinet Secretary. Then in June 1975, the Attorney-General brought two actions for injunctions to prevent the publication of the first volume and of further extracts by the *Sunday Times*. The Attorney-General argued that the courts should forbid publication as being contrary to the public interest. He also argued that there was a principle of law that no one should profit from the wrongful publication of information received in confidence. This principle had been recognized as a ground for restraining the unfair use of commercial secrets transmitted in confidence. And in *Argyll v. Argyll*[53] the same principle was applied to domestic secrets passing between husband and wife during marriage. On the basis of this decision in that case, the Lord Chief Justice concluded that when a Cabinet Minister received information in confidence the improper publication of such information could be restrained by the courts. In particular, he said,

> The expression of individual opinions by Cabinet Ministers in the course of Cabinet discussions are matters of confidence, the publication of which can be restrained by the court when this is clearly necessary in the public interest.

This was a new principle or, at least, the considerable extension of an older principle. When the Lord Chief Justice came to apply this to the case before him, he decided that in view of the lapse of time (nearly 10 years since the end of the period covered by the first volume of the diaries) he would not issue the injunctions asked for because he could not believe that publication would inhibit free discussion of the Cabinet in 1975.[54]

In the event, therefore, the first volume of the Crossman diaries was published. But more important was the establishment of the new rule of law that the courts have jurisdiction to determine when the public interest requires that Ministers shall not be permitted to disclose information. I am not suggesting that there should be no constraints on such publication. But hitherto the constraints, if they have not been imposed by the Official Secrets Acts, have been political. The principle established by this case enables the courts to determine what is in the public interest on a matter which is at the heart of the political system.

Official secrets may be protected by the courts under a rule which provides that the Crown may claim that certain documents should not be disclosed to a party engaged in litigation on the ground that the public interest would be harmed by their production. In the leading case of *Duncan v. Cammell, Laird*[55] the plaintiffs were the legal representatives or dependents of some of the 99 men who lost their lives when the submarine *Thetis* sank during tests in Liverpool Bay. The defendants were those who had built the submarine. The plaintiffs called for the disclosure of plans, specifications and other documents relating to the construction of the submarine and the First Lord of the Admiralty objected. The objection was upheld by the House of Lords. That the rule applies to a great variety of cases is shown by the decision of the Court of Appeal in *Wednesbury Corporation v. Ministry of Housing and Local Government*[56] when an objection was upheld to the disclosure of departmental briefs for the guidance of, and correspondence with, Ministerial inspectors who had held a local enquiry into a proposal by the Local Government Commission that five local authorities should be extinguished and included in larger county boroughs.

As a result of these and other cases, it had come to be assumed that the affidavit of the Minister concerned which claimed non-disclosure, so long as it was properly executed, could not be challenged in the courts. If he said that disclosure was not in the public interest, that was the end of the matter. But in *Conway v. Rimmer*,[57] the House of Lords held that there might be a clash between the public interest that harm should not be done to the nation or the public service by the disclosure of certain documents, and the public interest in the proper administration of justice. If this were so, the court could inspect the

documents and might override the Minister's claim —
though if the Minister's reasons were beyond the competence of the court to assess, the Minister's view would
have to prevail. The action in the case was brought by a
former probationary police constable against his former
superintendent for malicious prosecution and the documents included reports made by the defendant on the
plaintiff. In the light of the later decision on the Crossman
diaries, Lord Reid's comments at one point in his judgment are interesting and left no doubt where his sympathies
lay in the perennial conflict between the secretiveness of
Governments and people's wish to know what is being
done in their name:

> Virtually everyone agrees that Cabinet minutes and
> the like ought not to be disclosed until such time as they
> are only of historical interest. But I do not think that
> many people would give as the reason that premature
> disclosure would prevent candour in the Cabinet. To
> my mind the most important reason is that such dis-
> closure would create or fan ill-informed or captious
> public or political criticism. The business of government
> is difficult enough as it is, and no Government could
> contemplate with equanimity the inner workings of the
> government machine being exposed to the gaze of those
> ready to criticize without adequate knowledge of the
> background and perhaps with some axe to grind.

One result of this decision may have been that the
Crown's claim to non-disclosure is less frequently made
than in the past. Recent cases involving disclosure of
documents held by Customs and Excise have been decided
in opposite directions[58] but one decision of more public
interest is disturbing. Under the Gaming Act 1968, certi-
ficates of consent have to be obtained from the Gaming
Board for the running of bingo halls. R. applied and the
Gaming Board made certain enquiries from the police.
The assistant chief constable of Sussex replied in a letter,

a copy of which came into the possession of R. who laid an information against him alleging criminal libel. As a result the chief constable of Sussex and the secretary of the Gaming Board were both summoned to produce this letter. The Home Secretary objected to its disclosure. The House of Lords held

> that the public interest required that the letters should not be produced, since, if the information given to the Board was liable to be disclosed, it might be withheld and they would thereby be hampered in the discharge of the duty imposed on them by statute to identify and exclude persons of dubious character and reputation from the privilege of obtaining a licence to conduct a gaming establishment.

The argument of the House of Lords was based widely on the public interest, not on the particular position of the Crown. Lord Reid said: 'It must always be open to any person interested to raise the question' of the public interest and it was said that Parliament in passing the Gaming Act must have expected that the Gaming Board would be obliged to receive certain documents which no one would contemplate they had to divulge.[59] The difficulty in all this is, of course, that such decisions make it extremely difficult, often impossible, for a private citizen to challenge a 'confidential' report made about him by the police or other public authority. The 'proper functioning of the public service' can be bought at too high a price.

NOTES

1. [1942] A. C. 206. See also *Greene v. The Secretary of State for Home Affairs* [1942] A. C. 284.
2. (1850) 5 Ex. 378.
3. [1941] A. C. 378, 393.
4. Emergency Powers (Defence) Act 1939 s.1(2)(a). See R. J. Sharpe, *The Law of Habeas Corpus* esp. pp. 89-124.

5. [1917] A. C. 260.

6. *National Breweries v. The King* [1920] 1 K. B. 854.

7. [1920] 2 K. B. 305.

8. E.g. in *Nakkuda Ali v. Jayaratne* [1951] A. C. 66 and *Ridge v. Baldwin* [1964] A. C. 40.

9. *Re McElduff* (1971) 23 N.I.L.Q. 112; *Re Mackay* (1972) 23 N.I.L.Q. 113.

10. *Op cit*, pp. 123-4.

11. *Thomas v. Sawkins* [1935] 2 K. B. 249.

12. *Duncan v. Jones* [1936] 1 K. B. 218.

13. *Arrowsmith v. Jenkins* [1963] 2 Q. B. 561.

14. *Rice v. Connolly* [1966] 3 W. L. R. 17.

15. *R. v. Prager* [1972] 1 All E. R. 1114.

16. *R. v. Osborne* [1973] 1 All E. R. 649.

17. See for example the debate in the House of Lords on 14 February 1973 (338 H. L. Deb. col. 1546-59, 1564-1678).

18. *Alderson v. Booth* [1969] 2 W. L. R. 1252.

19. [1934] 2 K. B. 164.

20. *Ghani v. Jones* [1970] 1 Q. B. 693.

21. *Garfinkel v. Metropolitan Police Commissioner, The Times* 4 September 1971.

22. *Ealing London Borough Council v. Race Relations Board* [1972] A. C. 342.

23. For a discussion of the case see John Hucker, *The House of Lords and the Race Relations Act* (1975) 24 I. C. L. Q. 284.

24. *Charter v. Race Relations Board* (1973) A. C. 868.

25. *Dockers' Labour Club v. Race Relations Board* [1974] 3 W. L. R. 533; in *Race Relations Board v. Applin* [1975] A. C. 259 the House of Lords held that foster parents were concerned with the provision of facilities or services to a section of the public, i.e. the children.

26. On the 'club' cases, see now Race Relations Act 1976.

27. [1975] 1 W. L. R. 1686.

28. [1967] 2 Q. B. 617.

29. [1968] 2 All E. R. 145.

30. [1968] 3 All E. R. 163.

31. [1969] 2 Q. B. 222.

32. [1976] 1 W. L. R. 971.

33. [1972] A. C. 60.

34. See below, pp. 137-8.

35. See *Ex parte Azam* [1974] A. C. 18.

36. [1974] 1 W. L. R. 683.

37. *R. v. Secretary of State ex parte Mehta* [1975] 1 W. L. R. 1087.

38. *R. v. Secretary of State ex parte Phansopkar* [1975] 3 W. L. R. 322.

39. [1976] 3 W. L. R. 630.

40. [1976] 3 W. L. R. 725.

41. Now S. I. 1976 No. 1572 provides a partial remedy.

42. *R. v. Secretary of State ex parte Soblen* [1963] 1 Q. B. 829.

43. *Schmidt v. Home Secretary* [1969] 2 Ch. 149. In *Van Duyn v. Home Office* [1975] 2 W. L. R. 760 the Court of Justice of the European Communities held that the United Kingdom was entitled to exclude a scientologist on the grounds of public policy under the terms of the EEC Treaty.

44. Report of the Committee on Contempt of Court (Cmnd 5794) para. 1.

45. *Morris v. Crown Office* [1970] 2 Q. B. 114.

46. *R. v. Thomson Newspapers* [1968] 1 W. L. R. 1.

47. *A-G v. Mulholland* [1963] 2 Q. B. 477.

48. *A-G v. Times Newspapers* [1974] A. C. 273.

49. [1973] 1 Q. B. 710.

50. [1975] Q. B. 637.

51. In *Re F* [1976] 3 W. L. R. 813 the Court of Appeal held that where a newspaper published information about a ward of court, it did not commit contempt unless it knew that what it published was forbidden by law.

52. 681 H. C. Deb. col. 1417-8 (23 July 1963) modified by resolution in 839 H. C. Deb. col. 1589-1627 (28 June 1972).

53. [1967] Ch. 302. In *Fraser v. Evans* [1969] 1 Q. B. 349 the confidential report of the plaintiff, who was a public relations consultant to the Greek Government, came into the hands of the *Sunday Times*. The Court of Appeal refused to issue an injunction to prevent its publication on the ground that the person to whom the confidential duty was owed (i.e. the Greek Government) was not seeking the protection of the court.

54. *A-G v. Jonathan Cape Ltd*; *A-G v. Times Newspapers Ltd* [1975] 3 All E. R. 484.

55. [1942] A. C. 624.

56. [1965] 1 W. L. R. 261.

57. [1968] A. C. 910.

58. See *Norwich Pharmacal v. Customs & Excise* [1974] A. C. 133 and *A. Crompton Ltd v. Customs & Excise* (No. 2) [1974] A. C. 405.

59. *R. v. Lewes JJ. ex parte Home Secretary* [1973] A. C. 388.

Chapter 5: Property rights and the control of ministerial discretion

The attitude of the judiciary to legislation which seriously interferes with rights to the enjoyment of property – especially the ownership of land has traditionally been one of suspicion. These rights have long been protected by the common law (which means the judges) and changes brought about by Acts of Parliament have not always been welcomed. The constitutional position is clear: statutes override the common law and must be enforced. But the judges also have the duty to interpret the powers given by statutes and in that process of interpretation they may be unwilling to extend the powers beyond their literal meaning. Generalizations, however, are misleading. It is necessary to indicate some of the conflicts that have arisen, and the ways in which they have been resolved.

Housing in the 1930s

The period between 1918 and 1939 saw the development of housing legislation, particularly for slum clearance. Powers were given by Acts of Parliament to local authorities and to Ministers of the Crown to demolish slums and to acquire land compulsorily in order to do so. Compulsory acquisition was no new thing; the railway boom of almost a century before had seen much of it. But the housing legislation of the 1920s and 1930s resulted in the destruction of much private property in the public interest and compensation was limited where the houses destroyed were unfit for human habitation.

In *R. v. Minister of Health ex parte Davis*[1] the Court of Appeal held that an improvement scheme was invalid because it did not contain particulars for the development of the area once the site had been cleared, nor did it confer on the local authority an unrestricted power to sell or lease the areas. Lord Hewart C.J., in the Divisional Court, said he understood that 'the real substance of the complaint is that under the name, and the agreeable name, of an improvement scheme, this particular council is minded to acquire a slice of very valuable land in the heart of the city of Derby, not for any purpose of re-arrangement or reconstruction, but for the purpose, if and when the local authority thinks fit, of resale, and, of course, of resale at the highest obtainable price'. In *R. v. Minister of Health ex parte Yaffe*[2] the facts were similar but the Minister, in confirming the order, modified the scheme submitted by the local authority to conform with the decision in the *Davis* case. In *Yaffe's* case, the House of Lords, reversing the decision of the Court of Appeal, up-held the order. In the Court of Appeal, Scrutton L. J. said: 'The present Act enables a Minister to take away the property of individuals without compensation on certain defined conditions. In my view these conditions must be strictly complied with, and only the very clearest words can give final validity to an Order which does not comply with the prescribed statutory conditions.' There seems to be a somewhat different attitude behind the con-cluding words of Viscount Dunedin in the House of Lords: 'No one could possibly look at these proceedings without being convinced that they are a genuine scheme for sweeping away an insanitary area and replacing the old by new and sanitary houses. There is no trace of any oblique motive. I should have been very sorry had I felt it necessary to frustrate the scheme and allow the con-tinuance of the insanitary area for a longer period upon what, at most, was no more than a technical objection.' In his dissenting judgment, Lord Russell of Killowen, echoing Scrutton L. J., said that as the Act empowered a local authority 'to take away property compulsorily, and in many cases to pay for it less than full compensation', it was 'therefore essential that all the provisions leading up to the exercise of such a power should be strictly observed according to the language of the statute.'

The Housing Act 1930 amended the law to enable a local authority to sell or lease the land in a clearance or an improvement area. The same Act introduced the procedure of making application to the High Court if a person aggrieved wished to claim that the order was *ultra vires*. Swift J. was appointed to hear these applications and the first case was *Re Bowman*.[3] The judge dismissed the application but stated:

> When an owner of property against whom an order has been made under the Act comes into this Court and complains that there has been some irregularity in the proceedings, and that he is not liable to have his property taken away, it is right, I think, that his case should be entertained sympathetically and that a statute under which he is being deprived of his rights to property should be construed strictly against the local authority and favourably towards the interest of the applicant, inasmuch as he for the benefit of the community is undoubtedly suffering a substantial loss, which in my view must not be inflicted upon him unless it is quite clear that Parliament has intended that it shall.

In *Errington v. Minister of Health*[4] the now familiar question arose of the application of the rules of natural justice to the procedure whereby a local authority makes an order which is subject to ministerial confirmation (in this case a slum clearance order) with an opportunity for interested parties to make objections which normally cause the Minister to hold a local enquiry before he makes his decision. In this case the confirmed order was set aside by the Court of Appeal because, after objections had been made, the local authority and the Ministry had conferred in the absence of the objectors. Maugham L. J. said:

> It seems to me a matter of the highest possible importance that where a quasi-judicial function is being

exercised, under such circumstances as it had to be exercised here, with the result of depriving people of their property, especially if it is done without compensation, the persons concerned should be satisfied that nothing unfair has been done in the matter, and that *ex parte* statements have not been heard before the decision has been given without any chance for the persons concerned to refute those statements.

At common law, the landlord of unfurnished premises was under no duty to ensure that they were fit for human habitation or in a state of good repair.[5] Parliament intervened and the present statutory provision, originally enacted in 1909, requires that, for small houses where the rent is low, there shall be implied a condition that the house is at the commencement of the tenancy, and an undertaking that the house will be kept by the landlord during the tenancy, fit for human habitation.[6]

Over the years, the courts have imposed a series of restrictions, by way of interpretation, on this statutory condition. The first was that the condition or warranty applied only to the tenant and not to his family – neither his wife nor his daughter were protected. The second was that the implied covenant of fitness did not extend to those parts of the premises such as a common staircase which the landlord retained under his control. Thirdly, the rent limits, it was held, referred to the actual rent payable without any deduction in respect of rates or other outgoings which the landlord might have agreed to pay. Fourthly the statutory covenant was restricted to cases where the house was capable of being made fit for human habitation at reasonable expense. Fifthly, restrictions were imposed by the courts concerning notice from the tenant of the defects.

Such restrictions reflect the reluctance of the judiciary to interpret social legislation, when it affects the property rights of landlords, in favour of tenants. Decisions such as these show that the courts inclined to the view that in a conflict between the common law property rights of an individual and the statutory powers of a local authority to interfere with those rights, the benefit of any doubt in statute was to be given to the individual – and that this was particularly so if the statute gave less than full compensation to the individual. This is, indeed, often said to be a presumption to which judges should have regard in interpreting statutes. The idea that Parliament, in this field, was 'interfering' with the common law died hard. The remarks of Lord Hewart C.J. in the *Davis* case seemed to indicate that the local authority was acting improperly and in bad faith. It was perhaps at these remarks that Viscount Dunedin's rejection of any 'oblique motive' in *Yaffe's* case, was directed. The Minister of Health in moving the second reading of the bill which became the Housing Act 1930, said that the practice of confirming schemes like that put forward in the *Davis* case had been followed by the department for more than half a century, and had received, so everybody thought, the approval of Parliament.[7] The question of compensation, to which the courts attached much importance, is full of political implications but the Minister in 1930 thought that the basis had been settled in 1919 'by general acclamation'.[8] However that may be, the degree of compensation is a somewhat uncertain ground on which to found judicial presumptions.

The changes in judicial attitudes
The period of the 1939-45 war and the years which immediately followed show a marked change in judicial attitudes. The emergencies of the war made necessary the granting of wide powers to public authorities under Defence Regulations and the courts proved extremely reluctant to interfere with the exercise of these powers. Thus in *Carltona v. Commissioners of Works*[9] the appellants challenged the requisitioning of their factory by the Commissioners of Works on the ground *inter alia* that the Commissioners could not, on the facts, have come to the

conclusion that the factory should be requisitioned. Lord Greene M.R. in the Court of Appeal rejected this argument, saying,

It has been decided as clearly as anything can be decided that, where a regulation of this kind commits to an executive authority the decision of what is necessary or expedient and that authority makes the decision, it is not competent to the courts to investigate the grounds or the reasonableness of the decision in the absence of an allegation of bad faith.

So also where the Minister of Fuel and Power appointed a controller to take over the running of a colliery, the argument that there were no adequate grounds on which the Minister could have found that it was necessary to take control was dismissed by the Court of Appeal as being one which the Court had no competence to accept, all these decisions being vested in the Minister.[10]

Under an Act of 1944 empowering local authorities to make compulsory purchase orders for land where the Minister was satisfied that this was requisite for the purpose of dealing satisfactorily with extensive war damage, the city of Plymouth made such an order. Some owners of houses on the edge of the area sought to argue that the Minister could not, on the facts, have been so satisfied. But the Court of Appeal held that this was a matter for the Minister to decide and so long as he acted in good faith his judgment could not be challenged in the courts.[11] And, after the war, other wide and general powers of compulsory acquisition of land were upheld both under the Town and Country Planning Act of 1947[12] and the New Towns Act 1946.

The Stevenage New Town case[13] well illustrates the line that has to be drawn and the difficulty of drawing it. In 1946 the Minister addressed a public meeting in Stevenage, before the New Towns Bill had been passed, and made clear to a somewhat noisy gathering his intention to promote the building of a new town at Stevenage. Many months later, after he had confirmed his draft order designating the area as the site of a new town, his decision was challenged on the ground that he had shown bias by his speech at the public meeting and so had legally disqualified himself from being able to make the subsequent decision. The House of Lords rejected this argument and upheld the Minister, on the ground that he could not be said to be biased because he had a policy.

The highest point in this reluctance to intervene with governmental activities was reached in the mid-1950s when the House of Lords interpreted a statutory provision, which limited the courts' jurisdiction to review a compulsory purchase order on land, so broadly that even fraud by public servants was held not to entitle the owner to bring an action.[14]

From the early 1960s, the courts reverted to their former attitude and have become increasingly willing to review governmental activities on a variety of grounds; the reluctance of the 1940s and 1950s has disappeared. Indeed, most recently, the senior members of the judiciary seem to have become enthusiastically interventionist.

Under town and country planning legislation, any person who wishes to 'develop' his land – as building on it or extracting minerals or changing its use to a significant extent – must obtain permission from the local planning authority. If that authority refuses permission, or makes conditions which the applicant does not wish to be bound by, he may appeal to the Minister. Often a local enquiry follows, conducted by an inspector appointed by the Minister, and the Minister (or in less important cases the inspector himself) decides.

The operation of these provisions has frequently been challenged in the courts, often with success, Ministers and local authorities being overruled sometimes, for example, because the development was deemed to have been already authorized,[15] or because the conditions attached were unreasonable[16] or were not related to the use of the land.[17]

It is difficult to summarize the very extensive case law on the procedure and substance of housing and planning legislation. The courts have carved out for themselves areas where they are sharp in their scrutiny of the way public authorities exercise their powers. These include procedural defects where it appears that the individuals affected may not have had a full opportunity to make their case against the proposed restriction of their property rights. Here the courts have developed the rules of natural justice which seek to ensure that that case is properly heard and that the decision is taken on proper and relevant grounds. They have also been strict in their application of the statutory provisions generally. To take a few recent examples: Messrs Lavender and Son were gravel extractors and were refused planning permission by Walton and Weybridge Urban District Council. The Minister of Housing rejected the firm's appeal stating that it was his present policy that such land should not be released for mineral working 'unless the Minister of Agriculture is not opposed to working'. In this case that Minister was so opposed. The High Court held that the Minister had acted wrongly and that his decision should be quashed because he had inhibited himself from exercising a proper or any discretion and had, in effect, delegated his power of decision to the Minister of Agriculture, which he was not entitled to do.[18]

Another 'policy' decision was *Coleen Ltd v. Minister of Housing and Local Government*.[19] Tower Hamlets London Borough Council declared two rows of houses, which were in very bad condition, to be slum clearance areas. At the corner where the streets met was a modern building in good condition which the Council included in their compulsory purchase order as being, in the words of the Housing Act 1957, adjoining land the acquisition of which was 'reasonably necessary for the satisfactory development or use of the cleared area'. The Minister confirmed the order but the Court of Appeal quashed it on the ground that there was no evidence on which the Minister could have come to his decision, none having been adduced by the Council.

In *Gosling v. Secretary of State for the Environment*[20] a compulsory order for slum clearance was quashed because the Minister and his inspector appeared to have considered whether the land was 'reasonably necessary for securing a cleared area of convenient shape and dimensions' when what they should have considered was whether the acquisition of the land was 'reasonably necessary for the satisfactory development or use of the cleared area'. In *French Kier Developments v. Secretary of State for the Environment*[21] a Ministerial decision on a planning appeal was quashed because the reasons given were not 'clear and intelligible'.

One surprising decision in the opposite direction was that in *Westminster Bank v. Minister of Housing and Local Government*,[22] where the House of Lords refused to quash a Ministerial decision which upheld a local authority's refusal to give planning permission in circumstances which denied to the applicants a right to compensation to which they would have been entitled had the local authority proceeded differently. It is an accepted principle that a statute should not be interpreted so as to enable private property rights to be taken away without payment of compensation unless that is the clear meaning of the statute. Although the planning Acts made no express provision, Lord Reid held that it was the 'irresistible inference from the statute read as a whole' that compensation payable under a different statute was excluded.

In another slum clearance case, the local authority made a compulsory purchase order on the ground of the unfitness of the houses for human habitation due in part to settlement affecting walls and floors. The report of the Minister's inspector, following a local enquiry, recommended the confirmation of the order stating that the settlement seemed to be due to the foundations not having been dug deep enough. The Secretary of State confirmed the order but the House of Lords unanimously quashed it because the state of the foundations had not been referred to at the local enquiry and so no opportunity had been given to the owners to bring evidence to show that the foundations were not defective. The owners had not, said Lord Russell, been given 'a fair crack of the whip'.[23]

Similarly where Surrey County Council wanted to use their land as a gipsy caravan site and parish councils objected at a local enquiry, the Secretary of State granted permission but his decision was quashed on the ground that the County Council seemed to have changed its policy as to the number of other sites needed, without giving notice of this. So there was a risk that the parish councils might be prejudiced by not having had an opportunity to question the County Council on this issue.[24]

These and many other cases show the very keen scrutiny to which the courts subject housing and planning decisions and how, to an extent very similar to their attitude in the 1930s, they are prepared to set aside the decisions of public authorities wherever they consider there has been any departure from the stringent, largely judge-made, standards of procedure.

Squatting

The combination of considerable housing shortage, especially in London, and of a large number of vacant houses, both publicly and privately owned, led to a recurrence of squatting: that is of homeless persons (often families with young children) occupying those houses.[25] Such persons are trespassers and the owners of the properties normally have a civil right of action for their eviction. Until 1970 there was a procedural difficulty that possession orders could not be made against squatters if they were not named as parties nor attended court. But in 1970 new rules of court were made under which speedy possession could be given provided that the owner showed that he had taken 'reasonable steps' to discover the identity of the squatters even if those steps had been unsuccessful.[26]

So, as the authors of the NCCL booklet referred to above said, 'the courts dealt with the situation . . . by rewriting the rule book'. In an early case after this new rule, squatters pleaded necessity. Lord Denning said of a married man with two children, aged 5 years and 5 months: 'They stayed with friends for a little while, but then they were told to leave. They were desperate, he says. They had not any relatives to assist them. They went in desperation to the Housing Department. They could not help them. They were forced to walk the streets.' So they occupied empty property owned by Southwark London Borough Council which was scheduled for redevelopment at some indefinite time in the future. Lord Denning dismissed the pleas of necessity:

> If homelessness were once admitted as a defence to trespass, no one's house could be safe. Necessity would open a door which no man could shut. It would not only be those in extreme need who would enter. There would be others who would imagine they were in need, or would invent a need, so as to gain entry. Each man would say his need was greater than the next man's. The plea would be an excuse for all sorts of wrong-doing. So the courts must, for the sake of law and order, take a firm stand. They must refuse to admit the plea of necessity to the hungry and the homeless: and trust that their distress will be relieved by the charitable and the good.[27]

In *McPhail v. Persons Unknown*,[28] Lord Denning repeated these words. And, he added, 'The owner is not obliged to go to the courts to obtain possession. He is entitled, if he so desires, to take the remedy into his own hands. He can go in himself and turn them out without the aid of courts of law.' But Lord Denning hoped he would not take this course 'because of the disturbance which might follow'. Nevertheless, the legal position was clear.

My conclusion is that, when the owner of a house comes to the court and asks for an order to recover possession against squatters, the courts must give him the order he asks. It has no discretion to suspend the order. But, whilst this is the law, I trust that owners will act with consideration and kindness in the enforcing of it – remembering the plight which the homeless are in.

The argument is highly dubious since Lord Denning put it on a logical basis that will not stand. He said: 'Seeing that the owner could take possession at once without the help of the courts' – and that itself is in this context probably bad law – 'it is plain that, when he does come to the courts he should not be in any worse position.' The conclusion does not follow from the premise.

Counsel for the defendants tried to argue that there was a principle of long standing that the courts had power to issue an injunction, when it was equitable to do so, to restrain an owner from proceeding with his action at law or with the enforcement of his order. But Lord Denning cited a case in 1830 where some claimants had wrongfully turned a widow out of a house and got possession of it and quoted the then Lord Chancellor who said: 'This court will not interfere to support a possession so acquired.' As Lawton L.J. said in the present case, it was 'but another example of the difficulties and unpleasantness of administering the law as it is without fear or favour to any man'. Presumably this is especially so when you and your fellow judges have so recently made the law 'as it is'.

The interpretation of the rule was further tightened against squatters when it was decided that even if the squatter had entered the property with the consent of the person entitled to possession, that person or his successor in title (in this case Bristol Corporation) could evict the squatter summarily when the period of the consent ended.[29] In another case Lord Denning refused to agree that the powers of summary procedure under order 113 were to be interpreted strictly against the landlord. They were to be construed, he said, in relation to the mischief aimed at: that squatters went into premises and one could not find out who was there. It was sufficient if one did what one could to find out the names of those who were there and covered all other persons as being 'persons unknown'.[30]

It has also been held by the courts that an electricity board, which agreed to supply electricity but subsequently discovered the users were squatters, was entitled to disconnect the supply. The squatters, although ready and able to pay for the electricity, were not to be regarded as occupiers for this purpose though they are so regarded when required to pay rates or when their eviction is sought.[31]

Although Order 113 rule 2(2) is generally believed to have been made to deal with squatters in residential property, it has been applied to students 'occupying' administrative offices of a university. Five students, out of 200, were named and at the first hearing the judge held that the university had not taken reasonable steps to ascertain the names of the other students. But the Court of Appeal overruled him and Lord Denning said, 'The names of the ringleaders are enough',[32] thus diluting the rule still further.

In *R. v. Wandsworth County Court*,[33] a London borough council obtained an order for possession against four squatters but when the bailiffs arrived to execute the order they found the premises occupied by another person (with his four children) who had not been a party to the proceedings in court. The Divisional Court decided that, when an applicant had obtained a judgment for possession, bailiffs were entitled to evict any persons found on the premises.

Rule 3(2) of Order 26 of the County Court Rules provides that where the applicant has not identified every person in occupation of the land, the application shall, in addition to being served on any identified persons, be served by affixing a copy of it, together with a notice, on the main door or other conspicuous part of the premises.

119

In *Westminster City Council v. Chapman and Persons Unknown*,[34] the county court bailiff put the application in an envelope addressed to 'Peter Chapman and persons unknown' and put it through the letter box. Peter Chapman had left the house some time previously but the other occupants read the application and all attended the county court hearing where one of them unsuccessfully questioned the validity of the service. From the order for possession made by the county court this person appealed. The majority of the Court of Appeal held that though the rule as to the manner of service had not been complied with, the service had been effective. They dismissed the appeal. Sir John Pennycuick, before whom many of these cases on squatters had come, dissented. He said the court was concerned with a special procedure of wide application. 'Once one departs from the strict application of this rule, it seems to me,' he said, 'that a number of difficulties of proof might arise in other cases, and there is also, I think, the possibility of abuse.'

These decisions show a remarkable consistency of approach. The treatment of these Supreme Court rules, with only the most minor exceptions, and their interpretation, consistently lead to decisions which favour owners and disfavour occupiers. It is disingenuous of the courts to pretend that they are bound to follow the course they have chosen to follow, and the tears shed for the homeless, especially by Lord Denning, add insult to injury. What the courts should be seeking is to hold an even balance in interpretation. Yet every procedural defect is excused when it is the fault of the owners and every provision is interpreted strictly against the occupiers. Sir John Pennycuick's dissent just mentioned is an almost unique exception.

Perhaps the judicial approach is best exemplified by a decision of Oliver J. in 1975.[35] The question was the familiar one of whether reasonable enquiries had been made to ascertain the identity of the occupiers. He concluded that they had not. But he said:

To construe the rule as meaning that a prospective plaintiff must take every step open to him which was reasonably possible would not only put an intolerable burden on him, but would turn any proceedings under the rule into something of a lottery, a forensic game of snakes and ladders, since the plaintiff could never know until he came to court whether the court might not, prompted by the ingenuity of counsel, find some further step which was reasonably practicable which had not been taken . . . The Rules of the Supreme Court were the instrument through which the courts acted to secure justice, their servants not their tyrants.

The judge waived the 'irregularity' and made the possession order. And so a rule which was invented to overcome a difficulty of knowing who were the proper defendants, a rule which provided expressly that the procedure it sanctioned could be implemented only where 'reasonable steps' had been taken to discover the identity of the proper defendants, has been interpreted so as to give the courts the discretion to treat that safeguard as an 'irregularity' which can be waived. And the ground given for this interpretation is that the plaintiff would otherwise be overburdened and that clever counsel might lead their lordships into error. The rule may, by this interpretation, be manipulated to favour one side in the dispute and be treated not as a part of the law governing procedure but as a tool in the hands of the courts.

THE CONTROL OF MINISTERIAL DISCRETION

A modern starting point to the prevailing attitude of the courts is the extraordinary case of *Burmah Oil v. Lord Advocate*.[36] In 1942 on the day before the Japanese army occupied Rangoon, the installations of the Burmah Oil companies were, on the orders of the British General Officer Commanding in Burma, destroyed to prevent their falling into the hands of the enemy. Subsequently the companies claimed compensation at a level higher than that to which they would have been entitled – and which they were offered – had the loss occurred in Great Britain. Both Conservative and Labour Governments strongly resisted this but the House of Lords, by a majority of 3 to 2, decided that there was a common law entitlement to such compensation in these circumstances. The Government immediately passed the War Damage Act 1965, nullifying the Lords' decision.

The earlier distinction between those matters which fell within the Ministerial or local authority discretion and those which were within the competence of the courts to adjudicate on has become increasingly blurred. Certainly the courts today are much less reluctant to intervene in this area than they were. Thus in *Padfield v. Minister of Agriculture, Fisheries & Food*[37] milk producers from the south-east asked the Minister to appoint a committee of investigation, alleging that the price which they were paid by the Milk Marketing Board was too low having regard to transport costs. The relevant statute empowered the Minister to set up such a committee but in this case he refused to do so on the grounds that the complaint was unsuitable for investigation because it raised wide issues; that if the committee upheld the complaint he would be expected to make an order to give effect to the committee's recommendations; and that the complaint should be dealt with by the Board rather than by the committee of investigation. A majority of the House of Lords found these reasons insufficient and ordered the Minister to set up the committee. They agreed that he had a discretion under the statute whether or not to do so but said that he was not justified in refusing if the result was to frustrate the policy of the Act of Parliament. Lord Morris of Borth-y-Gest disagreed. In his view, the court could intervene only if the Minister (a) failed or refused to apply his mind to or to consider the question whether to refer a complaint to the committee or (b) misinterpreted the law or proceeded on an erroneous view of the law or

(c) based his decision on some wholly extraneous consideration or (d) failed to have regard to matters which he should
have taken into account. And he held that none of these
was the case.

The view taken by the majority was surprising as the
decision of the Minister not to intervene was clearly one
of policy.

The decision of the House of Lords in *Anisminic Ltd v.
Foreign Compensation Commission*[38] shows how, on
occasions, the courts will resist the strongest efforts of the
Government to exclude them from reviewing executive
discretion. The Foreign Compensation Commission was
empowered by statute to deal with claims to compensation
under agreements with foreign Governments. The plaintiffs
owned property in Egypt which they lost at the time of the
Suez crisis in 1956. The Commission made a provisional
determination that the plaintiffs had failed to establish a
claim according to the rules laid down under the statute.
The statute provided that: 'The determination by the
commission of any application made to them under this
Act shall not be called in question in any court of law.'

Despite these last words the plaintiffs applied to the
courts for an order declaring that the Commission had
misconstrued the rules. The House of Lords, not for the
first or for the last time, held that 'determination' should
not be construed as including everything which purported
to be a determination but was not, and so the court was
not precluded from deciding that the order of the Commission was a nullity. Looking at the way the Commission
had construed the rules, the House decided that the determination was a nullity.

Lord Morris of Borth-y-Gest again dissented. He agreed
that the courts could intervene if the question was whether
or not the Commission had acted within its powers or its
jurisdiction. But 'what is forbidden is to question the
correctness of a decision or determination which it was
within the area of their jurisdiction to make.'

This distinction has a long and respectable history. If

an Act of Parliament says that A (who may be a Minister or a Commission or a local authority or an individual) shall be the person to settle certain specified questions and that there shall be neither appeal to nor review by any other body or person (including the courts), then A's decisions are unchallengeable so long as (a) it is A, not another, who decides, (b) A decides those specified questions and not others and (c) A does not act in bad faith or with similar impropriety. The *Anisminic* decision goes much further than this and says in effect that A's decision can be set aside by the courts if they disagree with his interpretation of the rules which he is required to apply.

This extreme case of judicial interference with the powers of public authorities may be contrasted with the attitude of the Court of Appeal in *Secretary of State for Employment v. ASLEF*[39] *and others (No. 2)*.[40] The Secretary of State exercised his powers to apply to the NIRC under the Industrial Relations Act 1971 for an order requiring a ballot of trade union members to be held. This power existed where, as the statute provided, it appeared to him that there were reasons for doubting whether the trade union members, in taking part in industrial action, were acting in accordance with their own wishes. The trade union appealed against the order given by the NIRC. Lord Denning first considered how far the words 'If it appears to the Secretary of State' put his decision beyond judicial challenge. He said,

In this case I would think that, if the Minister does not act in good faith, or if he acts on extraneous considerations which ought not to influence him, or if he plainly misdirects himself in fact or in law, it may well be that a court would interfere; but when he honestly takes a view of the facts or the law which could reasonably be entertained, then his decision is not to be set aside simply because thereafter someone thinks that his view was wrong . . . Of course it is to be remembered here that we are concerned with a grave threat to the national economy. The steps that are proposed do not imperil the liberty, livelihood or property of any man. The issue is simply: should a ballot be held of the railwaymen to ascertain their views?

Lord Denning then turned to the claim that the Minister had acted improperly.

It is said that it must 'appear' to the Minister that there are 'reasons' for doubting whether the workers are behind their leaders: and that the Minister has given no reasons. We have been referred to several recent cases, of which *Padfield v. Minister of Agriculture, Fisheries and Food* is the best example, in which the courts have stressed that in the ordinary way a Minister should give reasons, and if he gives none the court may infer that he had no good reasons. Whilst I would apply that proposition completely in most cases, and particularly in cases which affect life, liberty or property, I do not think that it applies in all cases.

Lord Denning concluded that the proposition did not apply in this case and that there were reasons which a reasonable Minister could entertain and so there was no ground on which the court could interfere with the Minister's decision to ask for a ballot order. He was supported by the other members of the Court of Appeal. In the event the union leaders were wholly justified, as the result of the ballot showed, in their claim that there were no reasons for doubting that the industrial action was in accordance with the wishes of the workers.

A more curious case, also affecting Government policy, came before the Court of Appeal at the end of 1975. Until 31 March of that year the fee for a licence for colour television was £12 for twelve months. From 1 April it was increased to £18. So some people whose licences expired after 31 March took out new licences before that date paying £12 and so hoping to postpone the date from which they would have to pay £18. The Home Office as the responsible authority then required those persons to pay the extra £6 under threat that the new licences would be revoked. Eventually on 26 November 1975 the Home Office sent out notices to those who had not paid up revoking their licences with effect from 1 December.

The licence fee is fixed by regulations made under statute which also provides that a licence may be revoked, or the terms, provisions or limitations thereof varied, by a notice in writing of the Minister. The Court of Appeal held that this power to revoke could not properly be used for the purpose of forcing people who had lawfully bought £12 licences before 1 April to pay the extra £6. Lord Denning said: 'The licence was granted for 12 months and could not be revoked simply to enable the Minister to raise more money. Want of money was no reason for revoking a licence.' Indeed, said Lord Denning, the demands for £6 were made contrary to the Bill of Rights; they were an attempt to levy money for the use of the Crown without the authority of Parliament.

It has long been the tradition of the courts to interpret tax laws[41] in favour of the subject if there was doubt about their meaning. And advising on tax avoidance is a highly prosperous profession. Perhaps that tradition weighed with their Lordships. But it was a decision which showed how words which apparently gave a wide discretion to the Minister – to revoke licences – were given a closely restricted meaning by the courts.[42]

Two recent cases exemplify the recent greater willingness of the courts to control Ministerial discretion. In *Secretary of State for Education and Science v. Tameside Metropolitan Borough Council*,[43] the Minister acted under section 68 of the Education Act 1944 which provided:

If the Secretary of State is satisfied . . . that any local education authority . . . have acted or are proposing to act unreasonably . . . he may . . . give such directions . . . as appear to him to be expedient.

In March 1975 the Labour-controlled Tameside Council put forward proposals to the Secretary of State for the reorganization of secondary education along comprehensive lines to come into effect in September 1976. The proposals were approved in November 1975. The council made many of the necessary arrangements for the change-over and told pupils which schools they would be going to.

At the local elections in May 1976, the Conservatives won control of the council and on 7 June told the Secretary of State that they proposed not to implement the plans for the conversion of the five grammar schools into comprehensives and sixth-form colleges. On 11 June the Secretary of State gave the council a direction under section 68, requiring them to implement their predecessors' plans, and on 18 June the Divisional Court ordered the council to comply. On 26 July the Court of Appeal overruled the Divisional Court and on 2 August, moving with impressive speed, Lords Wilberforce, Diplock, Salmon, Russell and Dilhorne upheld the Court of Appeal.

The basis of their Lordships' decision was that the Minister could give a valid direction only if he was satisfied that no reasonable local authority could have decided as the Conservative majority did; and that he could not have been so satisfied.

The second case was that of the Laker Airways. Under the Civil Aviation Act 1971, the Civil Aviation Authority was empowered to grant licences to those wishing to operate air transport lines. The Authority granted a licence to Mr Freddy Laker for the period from 1973 to 1982 to operate a cheap passenger service known as 'Skytrain' between the United Kingdom and the USA. The Conservative Government supported the project but in February 1976 the Labour Government (which had previously supported Mr Laker), through its Secretary of State for Trade in a White Paper, announced a change of civil aviation policy.

The Act of 1971 empowered the Secretary of State to 'give guidance' to the Authority with respect to their statutory functions. The White Paper purported to contain such guidance which, in accordance with the Act, was approved by a resolution of each House of Parliament. The crucial phrase in the White Paper guidance was that the Authority should not licence more than one British airline to serve the same route, with British Airways as the preferred airline to the USA. That prevented Skytrain from coming into operation.

The Court of Appeal held that the power of the Secretary of State to give guidance to the Authority did not extend to such a discretion. Said Lord Denning M.R.:

> 'Guidance' could only be used to explain, amplify or supplement the general objectives or provisions of the Act. If the Secretary of State went beyond the bounds of 'guidance' he exceeded his powers; and the Civil Aviation Authority was under no obligation to obey him.

So Mr Laker succeeded in his action.[44]

These two cases while comparable are also dissimilar. In both cases two public authorities were in conflict. In *Laker*'s case the Minister was seeking to require the Civil Aviation Authority to follow his policy but he chose a way of doing this which the Court of Appeal considered not to be within his powers. Many Acts of Parliament define, in different words, the nature of the relationship between Ministers and public corporations. Often the Minister may give 'directions' – as indeed he could under another section of the Civil Aviation Act 1971 – or 'general directions' or even orders of one sort or another. But 'guidance' is a weak word and does not seem apt to enable a Minister to give what were in effect specific instructions. In *Tameside* the central Department and the local authority were in direct conflict over a matter of administrative feasibility. The Minister did not believe that Tameside council could properly implement the change within the limited time available.

The decision in *Laker* is much easier to accept than that in *Tameside*. The latter may be contrasted with *Aslef (No. 2)*[45] where the trade union's complaint that the Minister had no reason to believe that the members were not behind their leaders was not supported by the court. In *Tameside* the Minister had sound administrative reasons for believing that the local authority was acting unreasonably but it was held that merely to have such reasons was insufficient. A remarkable feature of this decision of the House of Lords was that it was based on almost no judicial authority at all. One of their Lordships referred to *Aslef (No. 2)*, and to one other decision. The other three referred to none. Yet this is hardly an area where judicial pronouncements have been lacking. It concerns the whole matter of judicial control over Ministerial discretion.

Professor de Smith[46] wrote that Parliament might purport to restrict judicial review by conferring powers in subjective terms, the public authority being entitled to act when it 'is satisfied' or when 'it appears' to it that, or when 'in its opinion', a prescribed state of affairs exists. Then the courts interpret such phrases so as to give themselves more or less control as they wish. This depends on the judges' views of the merits of the case before them or (I would add) the direction their political inclinations lead them – what I call below their view of the public interest.[47] If trade unions are being restricted by Ministerial action (as in *Aslef* [*No. 2*]) then statutory limitations on Ministers' powers will be interpreted loosely. If Ministers appear to the courts to be acting in a way which is arbitrary or unfair (as in *Padfield* and *Tameside* and *Laker*) then the limitations will be insisted on. Little attempt is made to treat like situations in a like manner or to act consistently within a framework of judicial analysis. And one is often left with a feeling that in this area of the law judges rely almost entirely on their own sense of justice or on their own, personal conception of what is best.

The most recent case in which the courts appeared to be in conflict with Ministers was *Gouriet v. Union of Post*

Office Workers,[48] in which the plaintiff sought an order from the court to restrain the defendant trade union from breaking the law by refusing to handle mail to South Africa. Usually, a person, like the plaintiff, who suffers no special damage from a breach of the law, must ask the Attorney-General either to institute proceedings or to give his consent (in a relator action) to the plaintiff's proceeding. In this case the Attorney-General refused to do either. One question that arose was whether this decision was subject to judicial review. Lord Justice Ormrod said that it was not. Lord Justice Lawton said that if the Attorney-General decided not to enforce the law, the court could not make him do so, nor could it make him reveal what his reasons were.

But Lord Denning took a different view. He said:

The Attorney-General tells us that when he refuses his consent, his refusal is final. It cannot be overridden by the courts. He is answerable to Parliament, and to Parliament alone. He declines even to give his reasons for his refusal. This is, to my mind, a direct challenge to the rule of law . . . Suppose that he refused his consent for corrupt motives, or in bad faith . . . or for party-political reasons, and not in the interests of the public at large . . . or because he considered that the information was laid by a pressure group, of which he disapproved . . . These instances are, of course, entirely hypothetical. I would not suggest for one moment that they existed here. But the possibility of them convinces me that his discretion to refuse is not absolute or unfettered. It can be reviewed by the courts. If he takes into account matters which he ought not to take into account, or fails to take into account the matters which he ought to take into account, then his decision can be overridden by the courts. Not directly, but indirectly. If he misdirects himself in coming to his decision, the court can say: 'Very well then. If you do not give your consent, or your reasons, we will hear the complaint of this citizen without it.'

But the House of Lords rejected this view. Lord Wilberforce said:

The distinction between public rights, which the Attorney could, and the individual having no special interest could not, seek to enforce, and private rights was fundamental in our law. To break it, as Mr Gouriet's counsel invited their Lordships to do, was not a development of the law, but a destruction of one of its pillars.

Lord Wilberforce went on to state the highly restricted view of the judicial function that executive decisions which 'were of the type to attract political criticism and controversy showed that they were outside the range of discretionary problems which the courts could resolve'.[49]

Clauses seeking to exclude the court's jurisdiction are sometimes accompanied by provisions which entitle an aggrieved person, on limited grounds, to apply to the High Court for an order which would quash the decision made by the public authority. This application is required to be made within six weeks of the decision. The reason for the short period is that the decision – particularly to acquire land compulsorily – should not be capable of being reversed except immediately. *Smith v. East Elloe R.D.C.* (see above p. 113) fell within this provision and some doubt was thrown on this decision by that in *Anisminic.* But in *R. v. Environment Secretary ex parte Ostler*[50] the Court of Appeal held that the strict rule still applied.

In *Ostler* the aggrieved person was a corn merchant who discovered too late, but without any failure on his part, that a secret agreement about a road scheme had been arrived at under which two local companies withdrew objections to the scheme on being given a 'guarantee' by an official of the Government Department concerned that the scheme would be amended subsequently – with the result that the merchant's premises and business would be injuriously affected. Because the agreement was secret, the merchant failed to object within six weeks. The Court was told that 80 per cent of the land had been acquired and 90 per cent of the buildings had been demolished. Said Lord Denning M.R.: 'It would be contrary to the public interest that the demolition should be held up or delayed by further evidence or enquiries.' Ostler failed in his action.

These decisions in *East Elloe* and *Ostler* operated harshly against the individual but the courts are caught in a dilemma not of their own making. Clearly, decisions taken by public authorities which will result in public works, such as building houses or improving roads, cannot be capable of being reversed after a period of years. So the period for challenge is short. But under the present law it is often impossible for the courts to give damages to an individual who has suffered irreversible loss in these circumstances. The remedy for that lies with Parliament.

NOTES

1. [1929] 1 K.B. 619.
2. [1930] 2 K.B. 98; [1931] A.C. 494.
3. [1932] 2 K.B. 621.
4. [1935] 1 K.B. 249.
5. See J. I. Reynolds, *Statutory Covenants of Fitness and Repair: Social Legislation and the Judges* (37 M.L.R. 377). For a view critical of this article, see M. J. Robinson 39 M.L.R. 43.
6. Housing Act 1957 s.6.
7. 237 H.C. Deb. col. 1807.
8. At col. 1814.
9. [1943] 2 All E.R. 560.
10. *Point of Ayr Collieries v. Lloyd George* [1943] 2 All E.R. 546.
11. *Robinson v. Minister of Town & Country Planning* [1947] K.B. 702.
12. *Earl Fitzwilliam's Estates v. Minister of Housing & Local Government* [1952] A.C. 362.

13. *Franklin v. Minister of Town & Country Planning* [1948] A.C. 87.

14. *Smith v. East Elloe R.D.C.* [1956] A.C. 736.

15. *Pyx Granite v. Ministry of Housing & Local Government* [1960] A.C. 260.

16. *Hall & Co. v. Shoreham-by-Sea* [1964] 1 All E.R. 1.

17. *Mixnam's Properties v. Chertsey U.D.C.* [1965] A.C. 735.

18. *H. Lavender & Son Ltd v. Minister of Housing & Local Government* [1970] 1 W.L.R. 123.

19. [1971] 1 W.L.R. 433.

20. (1975) J.P.L. 406.

21. *The Times* 25 October 1976; see also *Hope v. Secretary of State for the Environment* (1975) 31 P. & C.R. 120.

22. [1971] A.C. 508.

23. *Fairmount Ltd v. Secretary of State for the Environment* [1976] 1 W.L.R. 1255.

24. *Hambledon & Chiddingfold Parish Councils v. Secretary of State for the Environment* [1976] J.P.L. 502.

25. See National Council for Civil Liberties, *Squatting: trespass and civil liberties* (1976).

26. Orders 113 of the Rules of the Supreme Court and 26 of the County Court. Lord Denning as Master of the Rolls presided over the Court of Appeal and was a member of the Rule committee which introduced these changes.

27. *Southwark L.B.C. v. Williams* [1971] 1 Ch. 734.

28. [1973] 3 W.L.R. 71.

29. *Bristol Corporation v. Persons Unknown* [1974] 1 W.L.R. 365; *Greater London Council v. Jenkins* [1975] 1 W.L.R. 155.

30. *Metropolitan Police Receiver v. Smith* (1974) 118 S.J. 583.

31. *Woodcock v. South Western Electricity Board* [1975] 1 W.L.R. 983.

32. *Warwick University v. de Graaf* [1975] 1 W.L.R. 1126; for factory occupiers, see *Crosfield Electronics v. Baginsky* [1975] 1 W.L.R. 1135.

33. [1975] 1 W.L.R. 1314.

34. [1975] 1 W.L.R. 1112.

35. *Burston Finance v. Wilkins and Persons Unknown, The Times* 17 July 1975.

36. [1965] A.C. 75.

37. [1968] A.C. 997. Contrast *British Oxygen v. Minister of Technology* (1971) A.C. 610 where the House of Lords refused to interfere with a Ministerial discretion about investment grants.

38. [1969] 2 A.C. 147.

39. Associated Society of Locomotive Engineers & Firemen.

40. [1972] 2 Q.B. 455. The 'others' included the other railway unions.

41. See e.g. *R. v. Harz* [1967] 1 A.C. 760; *R. v. Churchill* [1967] 2 A.C. 224.

42. *Congreve v. Home Office, The Times* 5 December 1975.

43. [1976] 3 W.L.R. 641.

44. *Laker Airways Ltd v. Department of Trade, The Times* 16 December 1976.

45. See above pp. 124-5.

46. *Judicial Review of Administrative Action* (3rd Edn. pp. 318-20).

47. See Chapter 9.

48. Delivered by the Court of Appeal on 27 January 1977.

49. See *The Times* 27 July 1977.

50. [1976] 3 W.L.R. 288.

Chapter 6: The uses of conspiracy

I have already noted the importance of the crime and the tort of conspiracy in relation to trade unions, particularly in the late nineteenth and early twentieth centuries. More recently, criminal conspiracy has acquired a new significance in other fields.

The essence of the crime of conspiracy is an agreement between two or more persons to commit an unlawful act. The crime is the agreement and its execution or non-execution is irrelevant. Moreover the agreement may be inferred: 'A nod or a wink may amount to conspiracy.' But also it is not necessary that the conspirators should ever have met or known each other so long as there was evidence that they were acting in concert. Men may be selected at random from an extensive picket or well known individuals selected out of thousands who are demonstrating.[1] A single person may be charged with conspiracy 'with persons unknown'.

Moreover the unlawfulness of the act which the conspirators agree to commit is not limited to criminal acts. It extends widely to civil wrongs also, such as trespass on property and beyond that to an ill-defined area where it seems sufficient that the act is immoral or even a matter of public concern.[2] It follows therefore that a person may be convicted of conspiracy to commit an act for which he could not be prosecuted if he acted alone. The charge of conspiracy may also be used to avoid the necessity of some procedural requirement which attaches to the substantive act. Thus for some crimes – such as prosecutions under the Official Secrets Acts – the leave of the Attorney-General must be obtained. But conspiracy to commit an offence under those Acts does not require leave. Again, proceedings for certain specific offences – for example under the Obscene Publications Act 1959 – may be prohibited by statute but the prohibition does not cover conspiracy to commit those offences.

For various technical reasons, the rules of evidence apply much less strictly to proof of conspiracy, and it is common for prosecutors to add a charge of conspiracy to charges on the connected substantive offences. This enables the prosecution to indulge in 'plea bargaining', that is, in offering to drop the conspiracy charge if the accused will plead guilty to one or more of the substantive charges. Judges have objected to the adding of the conspiracy charges but in the case of the Shrewsbury pickets the Court of Appeal advanced a dangerous and prejudicial view. 'It is not desirable,' said Lord Justice James, 'to include a charge of conspiracy which adds nothing to an effective charge of a substantive offence. But where charges of substantive offences do not adequately represent *the overall criminality* it may be appropriate and right to include a charge of conspiracy.'[3] But how can this notion of 'the overall criminality' be determined?

As has been said, 'a conspiracy count puts the whole lifestyle of the accused on trial'[4] and this can very easily and adversely affect the minds of the jury with matters which are irrelevant to the charges.

Finally, and importantly, the penalties for conspiracy are in effect unlimited. The substantive offence may carry a maximum penalty of a few months' imprisonment. But if the accused is convicted of conspiracy to commit that offence he may be sentenced to many years' imprisonment. Trade unionists in the nineteenth century were frequently punished in this way. And most recently there has been a revival of the charge of conspiracy to intimidate so that one of the convicted Shrewsbury pickets was sentenced to three years' imprisonment on that charge whereas the maximum penalty for intimidation itself was three months.

The decision whether to prosecute, and if so on what charges, is normally a matter for the police or the Director of Public Prosecutions. In this sense the use of conspiracy in recent years is not the responsibility of the judges. But the extent of their willingness to encourage the development of the common law in this area is strongly influential on decisions about prosecutions and in the success of prosecutions, so we must consider what has been their attitude to the political and social aspects of this crime.

MORAL BEHAVIOUR

The Street Offences Act 1959 made it an offence, punishable by fine and, after more than one previous conviction, by imprisonment, for a prostitute to loiter or solicit in a street or public place for the purposes of prostitution. The effect of this statute was to prevent prostitutes soliciting in public. The accused published a booklet, the Ladies Directory, in which prostitutes inserted advertisements which they paid for. He was charged with, first, conspiracy to corrupt public morals; secondly, living on the earnings of prostitution; and thirdly, publishing an obscene article. His conviction on all three counts was upheld by the House of Lords.

With one dissentient the Law Lords held, against the vigorous denial of counsel for the accused, that there was an offence known to the common law of conspiracy to corrupt public morals. Viscount Simonds said:

I entertain no doubt that there remains in the courts of law a residual power to enforce the supreme and fundamental purpose of the law, to conserve not only the safety and order but also the moral welfare of the State, and that it is their duty to guard it against attacks which may be the more insidious because they are novel and unprepared for. That is the broad head (call it public policy if you wish) within which the present indictment falls. It matters little what label is given to the offending act. To one of your Lordships it may appear an affront to public decency, to another considering that it may succeed in its obvious intention of provoking libidinous

137

desires, it will seem a corruption of public morals. Yet others may deem it aptly described as the creation of a public mischief or the undermining of public conduct. The same act will not in all ages be regarded in the same way. The law must be related to the changing standards of life, not yielding to every shifting impulse of the popular will but having regard to fundamental assessments of human values and the purposes of society. Today a denial of the fundamental Christian doctrine, which in past centuries would have been regarded by the ecclesiastical courts as heresy and by the common law as blasphemy, will no longer be an offence if the decencies of controversy are observed. When Lord Mansfield, speaking long after the Star Chamber had been abolished, said that the Court of King's Bench was the *custos morum* of the people and had the super-intendency of offences *contra bonos mores*, he was asserting, as I now assert, that there is in that court a residual power, where no statute has yet intervened to supersede the common law, to superintend those offences which are prejudicial to the public welfare.[5]

This now famous statement was not universally applauded, many of those who disliked it being of the opinion that Law Lords were not necessarily the most appropriate persons to prescribe codes of moral behaviour (and to make them into rules of law also) for the rest of the community. Lord Reid's dissent was based on an examination of the history of criminal conspiracy (from its origins in the Star Chamber) and on 'the broad general principles which have generally been thought to underlie our system of law and government and in particular our system of criminal law'. He concluded that there was 'no such general offence known to the law as conspiracy to corrupt public morals'.

The judgments in the House of Lords were delivered on 4 May 1961. No further prosecutions for conspiracy to corrupt public morals were brought until 1965 in which year 77 persons were convicted and this was followed in 1966 by a further 45 convictions. In 1972, the Lord Chancellor said that most of the 32 cases (involving 134 individual convictions) between 1961 and 1971 were for 'blue' films which could not be proceeded against for obscenity unless shown in a private home.[6] So the conspiracy charge was used.

In 1971 three editors of *Oz* were charged with conspiracy to corrupt public morals by producing a magazine containing obscene articles, cartoons, drawings and illustrations; and with contravening the Obscene Publications Act 1964, and the Post Office Act 1953. On the conspiracy charge the jury acquitted them, not being satisfied that they intended to corrupt public morals. On other charges they were convicted and sentenced to imprisonment of 15, 12 and 9 months. On appeal these convictions were quashed except for that relating to the Post Office Act the sentence for which was automatically suspended. The appeals succeeded because it was held that the judge had misdirected the jury about the meaning of obscene in the Obscene Publications Act.[7] It was particularly in relation to this case that Mr Robertson drew attention, as I have already mentioned,[8] to the fact that the addition of a conspiracy charge enables the whole lifestyle of the accused to be brought before the court and the jury so that the case becomes politically charged in the sense that the accused can be subjected by prosecuting counsel to such allegations as advocating dropping out of society, living off the state, and regarding sex as something to be worshipped for itself.

The next year saw the prosecution of another magazine, *International Times*. Three directors were convicted of conspiracy (1) to corrupt public morals and (2) to outrage public decency, because they had published advertisements inviting readers to meet the advertisers for the purpose of homosexual practices. The House of Lords (with one dissentient) upheld the convictions on the first count, on the grounds either that the *Shaw* case was rightly decided, or that even if it were wrongly decided it should stand until altered by Act of Parliament. The Lords (with one dissentient) allowed the appeal on the second count, two of them on the ground that the offence of conspiracy to outrage public decency was an offence unknown to the law, and two of them on the ground that there had been misdirection by the judge; those latter two and the dissentient agreed that there was an offence of that nature.[9]

Lords Morris and Reid took part in the decisions of both *Shaw* and *Knuller*. Lord Reid had dissented in *Shaw* and had held there was no offence to corrupt public morals; but he was not willing to participate in overruling that decision when the same point arose in *Knuller*. He did, however, hold in *Knuller* that there was no offence of conspiracy to outrage public decency. Lord Morris had been with the majority in *Shaw* when upholding the conviction. And in *Knuller* he was the dissentient to allowing the appeal on the second count.

In the event therefore the decision in *Knuller* reinforced that in *Shaw*. But Lord Diplock in the former case was strongly critical of *Shaw* saying bluntly of that decision that he thought it was wrong and should not be followed. He said that Viscount Simonds's reasoning in *Shaw* had been anticipated in 1591 in Lambard[10]:

Is it not meet and just, that when the wicked sort of men have excogitated anything with great labour of wit and cunning, so as it may seem they have drawn a quintessence of mischief, and set the same abroach, to the remedilesse hurt of the good and quiet subject; Is it not meet (I say) that authoritie itself also, ... should straine the line of justice beyond the ordinarie length and wonted measure, and thereby take exquisite avengement upon them for it? Yea is it not right necessarie, that the most godly, honourable, wise, and learned persons of the land, should be appealed unto, that may apply new remedies for these new diseases.

It was not, said Lord Diplock, compatible with the development of English constitutional and criminal law over the past century that the House of Lords in its judicial capacity should assume the role of 'the most godly' etc. persons and take 'exquisite avengement' on those whose conduct was regarded as particularly reprehensible when Parliament had not found it necessary to proscribe that conduct and no previous precedent for punishing it could be found. As a result of *Shaw's* case, he said, it would seem that any conduct of any kind which conflicted with widely held prejudices as to what was immoral or indecent, at any rate if at least two persons were in any way concerned with it, might *ex post facto* be held to have been a crime.

In a case in 1973, twenty-one persons were charged with 43 separate specific offences relating to drugs. And then the 44th count alleged a conspiracy to corrupt public morals in that persons conspired together with other persons unknown to corrupt the morals of such persons as might consume heroin by procuring quantities of heroin and supplying the same to members of the public in and in the vicinity of Gerrard Street, London, W.1.[11] So it would seem that conspiracy to corrupt public morals may extend, as an offence, beyond the areas of sexual conduct and be used as a net to catch those who may be acquitted on other kinds of substantive charges. It should be added that if persons are convicted of a number of substantive offences the penalties can be severe because made cumulative; and that under the Misuse of Drugs Act 1971 the maximum punishment for the more serious offences (of which there are fourteen) is fourteen years' imprisonment. So it cannot be argued that the conspiracy is necessary to ensure that the penalties are severe.

DEMONSTRATIONS AND PROTESTS

In 1961, members of the Committee of 100 who sought to further the aims of the Campaign for Nuclear Disarmament took part in organizing a demonstration at an airfield which was a 'prohibited place' within the meaning of the Official Secrets Act 1911 and which was occupied by the US airforce. The plan was that some people would sit outside the entrances to the airfield while others would sit on the runway to prevent aircraft from taking off. The six accused were charged with conspiring to commit and to incite others to commit a breach of the Official Secrets Act, namely, 'for a purpose prejudicial to the safety or interests of the State' to enter the airfield. Their counsel was not allowed to cross-examine or call evidence as to their beliefs that their acts would benefit the State or to show that their purpose was not in fact prejudicial to the safety or interests of the State. They were all convicted, five of them being sentenced to 18 months' and one to 12 months' imprisonment. The Court of Appeal and the House of Lords upheld the convictions and sentences.[12]

The accused were not charged with any substantive offence, such as breach of the Official Secrets Acts (approaching or entering a prohibited place). No doubt, proof of conspiracy was easier.

In July 1972 Peter Hain appeared on charges of conspiracy to interrupt visits of South African sporting teams to Britain. The prosecution was brought by a private individual. He was convicted on one of the four counts, and fined £200. The count concerned his running on to a tennis court in Bristol during a Davis Cup match and distributing anti-apartheid leaflets.[13] It is not clear how far the conviction amounted to trespass (see below) but that was not the basis of the decision. It may be that any action which is 'a matter of public concern' can found an action for conspiracy. If so 'the agreement to commit an unlawful act' which is the definition of conspiracy may have been extended further.[14]

At present, however, another extension is of greater importance because it was created by a decision of the House of Lords as a deliberate statement of new law. The case concerned some students from Sierra Leone who occupied for a few hours part of the premises of the High Commission of Sierra Leone in London. They brandished an imitation gun and locked some ten members of the staff in a room. No blows were struck. Lord Hailsham said, delivering the opinion of the House of Lords, that the students

> appear to have been reasonably careful to see that no one was seriously harmed, and their motives were *not necessarily contemptible*. They acted from a genuine sense of grievance. The father of at least one of them was, we were told, under sentence of death at the time of the alleged offence, and all appear genuinely to have believed that the Government in power in their country, *though recognized by Her Majesty's Government here,* was *arbitrary, tyrannical and unconstitutional* [my italics].

The students were convicted of conspiring with other persons to enter the premises as trespassers.

Sit-ins and occupations, by students and factory workers, had for some time been troubling the courts and the legislators. As forms of protest, these were in varying degrees effective, especially if they received publicity and caused embarrassment. Normally they gave rise to no criminal action and the police were reluctant to intervene in what was seen as a private dispute on private property. From the beginning of student activity, however, there had been some who urged the introduction of legislation to enable such demonstrations to be dealt with as criminals. It was precisely this that the decision in this case achieved.

Lord Hailsham was a Lord Chancellor who chose to sit as a judge more frequently than is usual. On this occasion, he delivered the leading judgment with which two other Law Lords concurred (adding nothing) and the fourth concurred with a brief speech. Lord Hailsham was a highly political Lord Chancellor well known for his flamboyance and over-strained rhetoric. He lumped together in his political speeches:

> The war in Bangladesh, Cyprus, the Middle East, Black September, Black Power, the Angry Brigade, the Kennedy murders, Northern Ireland, bombs in Whitehall and the Old Bailey, the Welsh Language Society, the massacre in the Sudan, the mugging in the Tube, gas strikes, hospital strikes, go-slows, sit-ins, the Icelandic cod war.

The new rule of law he set forth in this case was:

> Trespass or any other form of tort can, if intended, form the element of illegality necessary in conspiracy. But in my view, more is needed. Either (1) execution of the combination must invade the domain of the public, as, for instance, when the trespass involves the invasion of a building such as the embassy of a friendly country or a publicly owned building, or (of course) where it infringes the criminal law as by breaching the statutes of forcible entry and detainer, the Criminal Damage Act 1891, or the laws affecting criminal assaults to the person. Alternatively (2) a combination to trespass becomes indictable if the execution of the combination necessarily involves and is known and intended to involve the infliction on its victim of something more than purely nominal damage. This must necessarily be the case where the intention is to occupy the premises to the exclusion of the owner's right, either by expelling him altogether . . . or otherwise effectively preventing him from enjoying his property.[15]

By this simple but considerable extension of the existing law, Lord Hailsham brought within the definition of criminal conspiracy, within its vagueness, and within its almost limitless powers of punishment, demonstrations of all kinds which involved either any entry into a public building or any use of property, whether public or private, which interfered (to however small an extent for however short a time) with an owner's enjoyment of any part of his property. Such an owner would be entitled to call on the police to enter the premises and make any arrests they thought appropriate because a criminal offence would be in the course of commission once two or more people appeared to be combining in such a demonstration. This decision is remarkable even for these authoritarian middle decades of the twentieth century. It also provides a very strong weapon for dealing as criminals with those who squat in empty buildings.[16] In the same case, the only other judge to speak (other than to concur) was Lord Cross. He went further even than Lord Hailsham saying that an agreement by several to commit acts, which if done by one would amount only to a civil wrong, might constitute a criminal conspiracy if the public had a sufficient interest. Such vagueness could lead almost anywhere.

The right to protest was further limited in *Hubbard v. Pitt*[17] in 1975. Lord Denning, MR, said that, some years before, Islington was 'run down in the world', with houses in a dilapidated condition, tenanted by many poor families. Then property developers stepped in, bought up houses, persuaded tenants to leave, did up the houses and sold them at a profit. Now they were occupied by well-to-do families. A group of social workers who deplored this development conducted a campaign. They accused the developers of harassing tenants and trying to make them leave. The social workers submitted various demands to local estate agents which, said Lord Denning, if tenants had been subjected to undue pressure, seemed reasonable enough. In the course of the campaign the social workers picketed the offices of Prebble & Co. About four to eight men and women stood on the pavement in front of Prebble's offices for about three hours on Saturday mornings, carrying placards saying 'Tenants Watch Out

Prebble's About' and 'If Prebble's In – You're Out', and handing out leaflets. They behaved in an orderly and peaceful manner and with the full knowledge and agreement of the local police. Prebble & Co. brought an action to stop these activities and Forbes J. granted an interim injunction from which the defendants appealed. In the Court of Appeal, two of the Lords Justices rejected the appeal on the technical ground that the interim injunction should be continued until the case was fully heard. As these cases are normally decided on the availability or otherwise of interim injunctions, this was an unrealistic view of the matter. Lord Denning, however, dissented from his two brethren, saying:

Here we have to consider the right to demonstrate and the right to protest on matters of public concern. These are rights which it is in the public interest individuals should possess; and, indeed, that they should exercise without impediment so long as no wrongful act is done. It is often the only means by which grievances can be brought to the knowledge of those in authority – at any rate with such impact as to gain a remedy. Our history is full of warnings against suppression of these rights. Most notable was the demonstration at St Peter's Field, Manchester in 1819 in support of universal suffrage. The magistrates sought to stop it. At least 12 were killed and hundreds injured. Afterwards the Court of Common Council of London affirmed 'the undoubted right of Englishmen to assemble together for the purpose of deliberating upon public grievances' . . . The courts . . . should not interfere by interlocutory injunctions with the right of free speech; provided that everything is done peaceably and in good order.

This is the voice of freedom under law. But on a technicality it was overridden by the other two members of the Court of Appeal.

In 1974 Lord Diplock said that on five occasions during

the previous three years the House of Lords had had to consider 'the protean crime' of conspiracy under one or other of the various shapes it assumed. The one he was considering was *R. v. Withers*[18] in which two husbands and their wives were charged with conspiracy 'to effect a public mischief'. Their actions had been to pretend, for the purposes of their enquiries as an investigating agency, that they were bank employees seeking information from other banks or building societies; and other similar deceptions. The other four cases were *D.P.P. v. Bhagwan*[19] the *Knuller* and *Kamara* cases and a case argued with *Withers*. Lord Diplock said:

In each of these five cases what was proved against the defendant at the trial was that he had done something of which the judge and jury strongly disapproved. In each of them what the defendant did was not itself a criminal offence whether done by him alone or in conjunction with other persons – or, if it was, that was not an offence with which he was charged . . . It would be disingenuous to try to conceal my personal conviction that this branch of the criminal law of England is irrational in treating as a criminal offence an agreement to do that which if done is not a crime and that its irrationality becomes injustice if it takes days of legal argument and historical research on appeal to your Lordships' House to discover whether any crime has been committed even though the facts are undisputed.

In *Withers*, the House of Lords concluded that the law knew no such generalized offence as conspiracy to effect a public mischief. This decision at least stemmed the attempt to spread the tentacles of conspiracy yet further. Viscount Dilhorne said:

The preferment of charges alleging public mischief appears to have become far more frequent in recent years. Why this is, I do not know. It may be that it is

147

due to a feeling that the conduct of the accused has been so heinous that it ought to be dealt with as criminal and that the best way of bringing it within the criminal sphere is to allege public mischief and trust that the courts will fill the gap, if gap there be, in the law. But if gap there be, it must be left to the legislature to fill.

The increased frequency is due, in part, to that climate of opinion in recent years which shows such animosity to deviations from social and sexual behaviour regarded as normal. It is through such cases that conspiracy has flourished. Thence it has been applied to cases of ordinary criminality.

The animosity seems to be primarily reactionary. That is, there has been in the last 20 years, especially by the younger generation, more disregard for conventional behaviour, more changes of sexual and social *mores,* more rejection of mainstream politics, than in any period since the 1920s. And this development has been more widely spread amongst all social classes than during that earlier period. The animosity has been in reaction to all this.

If the accused in *Withers* had been charged with conspiracy to defraud they might well have been convicted and the convictions upheld by the House of Lords. The prosecution overreached itself in framing the charges as public mischiefs. But if those charges had been upheld, the way would have been opened to almost limitless charges of conspiracy concerning 'immoral' behaviour. It would be most unwise to regard *Withers* as a turning of the tide.[20]

NOTES

1. See generally Geoff Robertson, *Whose Conspiracy?* (N.C.C.L. 1974); Robert Hazell, *Conspiracy and Civil Liberties* (Occasional Papers on Social Administration 1974).
2. See below p. 141. This vagueness means that the definition of the crime is for the courts to determine.
3. *R. v. Jones* (1974) *I.C.R.* 310 (my italics).
4. Robertson *op. cit.*, p. 42.
5. *Shaw v. D.P.P.* [1961] 2 W.L.R. 897.
6. See 333 H.L. Deb. col. 1569; and 839 H.C. Deb. col. *263-4, 427-8.* See also *The Law Commission* Working Paper No. 57 pp. 35-9.
7. *R. v. Anderson* [1971] 3 W.L.R. 939.
8. Above, p. 136.
9. *R. v. Knuller* (*Publishing etc.*) *Ltd* [1972] 3 W.L.R. 143.
10. *Lambard Archeion* (1635 ed.) pp. 86, 87.
11. See Hazell *op. cit.*, p. 33; *New Statesman* 23 February 1973.
12. *Chandler v. D.P.P.* [1962] 3 W.L.R. 694.
13. *Hain v. D.P.P., The Times* 28 July – 22 August 1972. Robertson *op. cit.*, p. 16 and Derek Humphry, *The Cricket Conspiracy*.
14. In *Cozens v. Brutus* [1973] A.C. 854, the House of Lords held that running on to the Centre Court at Wimbledon during a tennis match and distributing anti-apartheid leaflets was not 'insulting behaviour within the meaning of the Public Order Act 1936'.
15. *Kamara v. D.P.P.* [1973] 3 W.L.R. 198.
16. See above, pp. 116 *et seq.*
17. [1975] 3 W.L.R. 201.
18. [1974] 3 W.L.R. 751.
19. [1972] A.C. 60 (see above, p. 94).
20. For views of the Law Commission on conspiracy see Working Papers No. 50, 54, 56, 57, 63.

Chapter 7: Students and trade union members

Although student protest of one sort and another has a history as long as universities themselves, the 1960s saw a striking revival. Sometimes the protest was political and concerned events in the outside world. Sometimes it was directed against the way universities were organized and administered and most of the litigation before the courts arose from this cause.

Universities, being charitable corporations, are subject to the powers of their Visitor. This person will often be named in or under the charter establishing the university. Often he is the sovereign (in effect the Privy Council); and the sovereign is deemed to be the Visitor if no person is appointed. One function of the Visitor is to settle disputes between members of the university and to correct abuses and irregularities. Precisely which persons and what matters fall within the jurisdiction of Visitor is not easily definable but persons and matters within the definition are normally excluded from the jurisdiction of the ordinary courts. Some of the cases which have been heard by the courts (for example *R. v. Aston University Senate* which is discussed below) should perhaps have come before the Visitor.

Two cases show this limitation on the power of the courts to intervene (not that they have shown any wish to press their claim on these matters). In *R. v. Dunsheath ex parte Meredith* (1951),[1] the chairman of Convocation (the body of graduates of the University of London) refused to call an extraordinary meeting of Convocation, which was requisitioned by 79 members, on the ground that the motion to be discussed concerned not the University as such but only a college, the School of Slavonic and East European Studies. The motion deplored a decision of the Council of that School not to renew the appointment of a teacher and referred to 'widespread suspicion' that the reason for the decision was the teacher's membership of the Communist Party. When the High Court was asked to order the chairman to convene the meeting, the court refused on the ground that the matter was essentially one for the Visitor because it was a domestic question.

Similarly in another case, a law student claimed damages for negligence against the University for what he claimed was misjudgment of his examination papers. His argument (which he presented himself) was not sympathetically received. 'In his statement of claim,' said Lord Justice Diplock, 'the plaintiff set out a good deal of praise of his ability as a lawyer.' The action, said the Lord Justice, was 'wholly misconceived' and again the basis of the judgment was that this 'domestic dispute' was one for the Visitor and not for the courts.[2]

In 1718, Dr Richard Bentley, a member of the University of Cambridge was ordered to appear before the university court. But he refused 'contemptuously' saying the vice-chancellor was not his judge. Whereupon he was deprived of his degrees because of his words. So Dr Bentley went to the ordinary courts who ordered that his degrees be restored to him because the University could deprive him only for a reasonable cause which was not shown in this case.

Dr Bentley had not been given notice that the university court was to hear his case so he could not defend himself and that was a fatal flaw in the proceedings for 'even God himself did not pass sentence upon Adam, before he was called upon to make his defence'.[3]

The courts can generally be appealed to by anyone who considers that a decision has been taken against him which ought to have been taken in accordance with the rules of natural justice but was not. These rules at the least require that a person be told the case against him and be given an opportunity to refute it. If the rules of natural justice are not followed in circumstances where they should be, then the remedy given by the courts will be to quash the decision or to declare that it is invalid. But this remedy may be withheld by the courts even where they are satisfied that the rules of natural justice have not been complied with because the giving of the remedy is said to be at the discretion of the courts. This means that the person complaining may completely establish his complaint and yet the decision may not be quashed because a court does not think he 'deserves' to win. Obviously this ultimate power to withhold the remedy can give rise to feelings of injustice and to accusations that the courts are biased against individuals or particular groups of individuals.

The leading case on the rules of natural justice in recent times concerned the chief constable of the borough of Brighton. In October 1957 he was arrested and charged, together with other persons, with conspiracy to obstruct the course of justice. In February 1958 he was acquitted by the jury but the judge in passing sentence on two police officers who were convicted said that the facts admitted in the course of the trial 'establish that neither of you had that professional and moral leadership which both of you should have had and were entitled to expect from the chief constable'. The judge also remarked on the need for a leader in Brighton's police force 'who will be a new influence and who will set a different example from that which has lately obtained'. Soon after this the watch committee of the borough (the police authority) dismissed the chief constable without giving him a hearing or informing him of the charges against him. The House of Lords held that the dismissal was null and void. Lord Reid said that in cases where there must be something against a man to warrant his dismissal, he could not lawfully be dismissed without first being told what was alleged against him and allowed an opportunity to present his defence or explanation.[4]

When we look at the way the courts have dealt with

cases involving students, however, it seems that the narrowest possible interpretation has been applied to the rules of natural justice. In a case from Ceylon, after a student had sat for his final examination for B.Sc., an allegation was made by a fellow student to the Vice-Chancellor of the University that the student had had prior knowledge of part of a paper. A commission of enquiry found the allegation substantiated and the student was suspended indefinitely from all the examinations of the University. The student went to the courts in Ceylon to have the suspension set aside on the ground that evidence of several witnesses, including that of the fellow student who made the allegation, was taken in his absence, and that he was not aware of this evidence or of the case he had to meet.

The Supreme Court of Ceylon found in his favour because 'the procedure adopted was unfair to the plaintiff in that it deprived him of a reasonable opportunity of testing the truth of the case against him or of presenting his defence and explaining various matters in regard to which adverse inferences were drawn against him'. The decision was reviewed by the judicial committee of the Privy Council. The student did not appear and was not represented, apparently because he could not afford to do so. The Privy Council reversed the decision of the Supreme Court of Ceylon. They agreed that the commission of enquiry was bound by the rules of natural justice but held that these did not require the student to be present when witnesses were called. They said that a fair opportunity was given for the student to correct or contradict any relevant statement. The crucial issue was whether the student should have been provided with an opportunity to question the fellow student who made the allegation. As the Privy Council said: 'she was the one essential witness against the plaintiff, and the charge in the end resolved itself into a matter of her word against his.' But the Privy Council concluded that the absence of this opportunity was not an omission sufficient to invalidate the proceedings of the commission. Their Lordships said that this lack of opportunity to question the fellow student 'might have been a more formidable objection if the plaintiff had asked to be allowed to question [her] and his request had been refused . . . There is no ground for supposing that if the plaintiff had made such a request it would not have been granted.'[5]

This was a remarkable position for the Privy Council to take up. The rules of natural justice exist to ensure that proceedings are fair, and it is the responsibility of the authorities conducting the proceedings to see they are fair. To say that because the person alleging unfairness failed to insist on a fair procedure being followed he must suffer the consequences of the unfairness is a singularly crude and inequitable way of absolving those authorities from blame.

An even more remarkable interpretation of the rules of natural justice, as applied to students, concerned a teacher training college. The rules of the college provided, amongst other things, that the director of education for the local authority or his representative should be entitled to attend every meeting of the governing body of the college; and that the principal of the college was empowered to suspend a student for good cause, to report any such action to the chairman of the governing body and to refer the case to a disciplinary committee. This committee consisted of three members each of the governing body, staff and students. All findings of the disciplinary committee were to be referred to the governing body for approval.

Miss W was a student at the college. She, and four other women students, were found one night to have men in their rooms in the hall of residence in breach of the rules of the college. Later that morning the principal saw Miss W and told her that it might be better if she left the hall as soon as she could find other accommodation. Six days later, Miss W moved to lodgings in the town.

It appeared that the man had been with her for nearly

two months. The story got into the press and Miss W made statements which were reported. Two hundred students at the college signed a petition saying they had on one or more occasions broken the terms of occupancy. Said Lord Denning in later proceedings before the Court of Appeal: 'Many parents were worried lest their own daughters and sons were doing this sort of thing. It was all very bad for the college.'

The principal decided that she would not refer any of the cases to the disciplinary committee and, under the rules, she was the only person who could do so. But the governing body wanted disciplinary action to be taken. So they amended the rules to enable them to refer cases to the disciplinary committee; they then applied the amended rules retrospectively to the students concerned; and they fixed a date for the hearing before the disciplinary committee.

When the disciplinary committee met they were joined by Mr N who was an assistant education officer of the local authority and he stayed with the committee when they considered what their decision should be. The other students were reprimanded and some were required to leave the hall of residence. But Miss W was 'expelled from the college forthwith', and the governing body approved this decision. Miss W thereupon asked the courts to declare that her expulsion was invalid. She argued first that the governing body had no right to change the rules and to refer her case to the disciplinary committee. Apart from what might be regarded as an unfairness in changing the rules so as to enable the principal to be overruled, the difficulty of the amendment was that the governing body had put themselves in the position of appearing as prosecutor and judge. In particular the three members of the governing body who sat on the disciplinary committee would be involved, first, in referring the cases to the committee; second, in hearing the cases in the committee; and third, in approving the recommendation of the committee. To speak mildly, justice would not manifestly appear to be done by such a procedure. But Lord Denning was apparently unmoved by such arguments: 'We have seen the minutes,' he said. 'These show that the governing body, when they decided to refer these cases, were careful not to discuss the merits of any individual case' and with this Lord Denning was satisfied. Nor was he worried about the retrospective aspect. This he said was 'a matter of procedure only'.

What of Mr N's presence with the committee, especially when they were considering their decision? He was no silent spectator of their deliberations.

Mr N said he considered that Miss W's apparent lack of concern merited more severe treatment than the others. It was a serious offence and Miss W had knowingly flouted the regulations over a long period.

The affidavit in the case shows that he also

stated that he had been in touch with the Department of Education and Science and they viewed the matter with concern. He also stated that, because of the press report, the college had been made to look fools.

Lord Denning accepted that 'in general no person ought to participate in the deliberations of a judicial or quasi-judicial body unless he was a member of it . . . Nor should he retire with them for their deliberations lest this gives the impression that he is taking part in their deliberations when he is not entitled to do so, for then justice would not be seen to be done.' But Lord Denning thought that the rule that the director of education or his representative was entitled to attend every meeting of the governing body or its committees 'was wide enough to cover the disciplinary committee'. Moreover, said Lord Denning, 'he only drew attention to the obvious' and 'no harm was done by what he said'.

It is doubtful whether the disciplinary committee was a

committee of the governing body. It certainly included persons who were not governors. Moreover the principle that justice must not only be done but must be seen to be done overrides the argument that N did 'no harm'. And did 'the obvious' include N's report of what some official in the Department thought? Anyone who has any experience of governing bodies knows how susceptible they are to the view that they are made to look fools. In its effect, N's intervention was highly prejudicial to the question of what punishment should be administered to Miss W.

Even Lord Denning was unhappy about what had happened. He thought that in future 'it would be better for the director of education not to participate' in the disciplinary committee's deliberations and recommended that the rules should be amended accordingly.

In the meantime, of course, Miss W was to be expelled and her career ended. Lord Denning should be allowed the last word :

Instead of going into lodgings she had this man with her, night after night, in the hall of residence where such a thing was absolutely forbidden. That is a fine example to set to others! And she a girl training to be a teacher! I expect the governors and the staff all thought that she was quite an unsuitable person for it. She would never make a teacher. No parent would knowingly entrust their child to her care.[6]

A different kind of unreality descended on the Court of Appeal in *Herring v. Templeman*.[7] H was a student at a teacher training college. The trust deed of the college provided that the academic board might make recommendations to the principal for the dismissal of students whose standard of work was unsatisfactory; the principal had power to recommend dismissal; and any such recommendation was required to be confirmed by the governing body after considering such representations in writing or in person as the student might wish to make. In this case the academic board sent to the governing body an adverse report on H and this was the only document before the governing body. He was given a copy of this report ten days before the meeting of the governing body, attended the meeting, and was invited to give his reasons why he should not be dismissed. The governing body then accepted the recommendation from the academic body. H asked the courts to set aside his dismissal on the grounds that he should have been accorded a hearing by the academic board before it recommended his dismissal because it took into account extraneous matters going beyond his marks and grades; that he should also have had a hearing by the principal; and that the governing body should not have refused to re-open the academic board's assessment or to allow witnesses to be called or to reveal to H all the evidence, opinions, and reports on which the academic board had based its report.

The Court of Appeal held that there was no obligation on the academic board to give a hearing as it had the power only to make recommendations; that the principal was under no obligation to hold a hearing; and that the governing body had done all it was required to do. Lord Justice Russell, giving the judgment of the Court, said that he could see no reason why the academic board should hear the student 'before reaching a conclusion which when reached did not finally determine the student's future, for that matter had still to go to the principal and thereafter, if, but only if, he thought fit, to the governing body'.

It is easy to agree with the Lord Justice that there is not and should not be any obligation for the proceedings before the academic board and the principal to be conducted 'as if the parties were litigants before a court or before a legal arbitrator'. And indeed it is also strongly arguable that there was no obligation on the governing body to reopen the whole issue. But the reality of the proceedings was that the student was unable to present his case at any time when it might have genuinely affected the decision. The principal was (as is usual) the chairman of the academic board and his role would be primarily exercised in that body. It was the decision of the academic board, albeit in the form of a recommendation only, that was in effect conclusive. It would have been highly improbable that the principal would seek to overrule the board and even more improbable that the governing body would overrule the joint recommendation of academic board and principal. If therefore the rules of natural justice were to bite at all they could do so only by requiring a hearing for the student before the board. If the principle were to become established that bodies which recommend but do not decide are not bound by those rules, they would cease to be effective over a very wide range of procedures.

Reference has already been made to the discretionary power which courts exercise in deciding whether or not to give certain remedies. As these are remedies normally sought in cases alleging a breach of the rules of natural justice, this power often is crucial.

The facts in *Brighton Corporation v. Parry*[8] were similar to those in the case just discussed. P was a student at a teacher training college. The rules provided for the appointment of a disciplinary committee with a right of appeal to the governors or to an appeals committee nominated by them. The disciplinary committee had power to suspend or expel a student and he was to be 'afforded the opportunity to appear and to be heard, and be represented by a friend before any meeting of the disciplinary committee' at which his case was to be considered. He also had the same rights of being heard and represented before the governors or their appeals committee. Another rule stated that the academic board had power to exclude a student on academic grounds, with a right of appeal to the governors or the appeals committee. It was not stated that the student had any right to be heard or represented before the academic board.

P was elected about June 1971 as president of the students' union for the ensuing academic year. During that year of office (the 'executive year') he was expected to undertake a reduced amount of academic work 'in accordance with the requirements of the principal', and his course would be extended by a full year. Arrangements were agreed for this academic work, and two tutors were assigned to P for this purpose. As president, P was an *ex officio* member of the academic board.

In December 1971, the academic board considered progress reports on six students of whom P was one. P withdrew from the meeting under protest when the report on him was considered. The board required P to submit two pieces of work by 11 January 1972. This he failed to do and he also failed to fulfil other tutorial commitments. The deputy principal asked for an explanation. P told him that he 'had not had the time' and indicated that he did not accept the binding nature of this academic commitment as a student. He took the view that his sole responsibility was to the students' union. He stated that he thought it was important for the president to do some academic work 'although it is important that this is not seen as an element of control by the college authorities'. In February the academic board again insisted that he submit work – by March 16 – and said that if he did not 'the board would appear to have no choice but to exclude' P from the college on academic grounds. Further communications followed between the principal, the academic board and P. And P was excluded with effect from 25 March 1972. He appealed to the governors.

On 20 April after a long hearing at which P and the academic board were represented and witnesses were called on both sides, the appeals committee decided that P should be rusticated for the remainder of that academic year, thereby ceasing to be president of the students' union, but being eligible to return in September 1972 to continue his course. P however continued to act as president and claimed a right to attend meetings of the academic board. 'In other words,' said Mr Justice Willis in the High Court, 'despite what might be thought to have been a benevolent decision by the appeals committee, he has deliberately defied the college authorities, who have now sought an injunction to compel him to comply with their order.' The judge held that there had been no breach of the rules of natural justice because P 'knew precisely the nature of the complaints which were made about him', and was given an opportunity to state his case. The appeals committee acted in good faith. The judge then considered whether he should grant the injunction. In his view

such hardship as may be involved in granting the injunction is far outweighed by the likely consequences of refusing it. [P had acted] in plainest defiance of the authority of the college . . . He must have known that any college, which was not going to abdicate its authority in the face of a student challenge of that sort, would be bound to find such conduct quite intolerable . . . This is a case where the plaintiffs are entitled to look to the court to support them when their authority is deliberately flouted by an insubordinate student, particularly when that student is president of the students' union.

He granted the injunction.

Perhaps the most important of this group of cases is *R. v. Aston University Senate ex parte Roffey*.[9] Two students, R and P, were reading for the B.Sc. They failed an examination in subsidiary subjects in both June and September 1967. The examiners in those subjects and two of the course tutors, one of whom was chairman of the relevant examining boards, met on 19 September, considered the marks (which showed an unprecedented number of failures) and took into account personal and family difficulties. They decided that six students, including R and P, should be asked to withdraw from the course and letters were sent to them on 20 September. Between that date and 8 December 1967, several bodies considered the matter on several occasions and arrived at divers recommendations: the students' guild, the vice-chancellor, the dean of the faculty of social science, the board of examiners for behavioural science, the board of the faculty of social science, and the senate. 'No doubt,' said Mr Justice Donaldson, 'their interventions were inspired by the most laudable of motives, although their lack of unanimity was in many ways unfortunate.' Eventually on 1 November the Senate resolved to confirm the original decision of 19 September. The University Council met on 8 December, confirmed the Senate's decision, and 'resolved to defend the University against any attack and to issue a public statement'.

P and R applied to the courts, seeking the quashing of the decision to expel them. Mr Justice Donaldson said that the examiners

considered a wide range of extraneous factors, some of which by their very nature, for example personal and family problems, might only have been known to the students themselves. In such circumstances and with so much at stake, common fairness to the students, which is all that natural justice is, and the desire of the examiners to exercise their discretion upon the most solid basis, alike demanded that before a final decision was reached the students should be given an opportunity to be heard either orally or in writing, in person or by their representatives as might be most appropriate. It was, in my judgment, the examiners' duty and the students' right that such audience be given. It was not given and there was a breach of the rules of natural justice.

Mr Justice Blain also thought that 'common fairness demanded an opportunity for representation to be made' by or on behalf of P and R, though not necessarily in a personal interview. Lord Parker C.J. was 'not prepared to differ from the conclusion that there has been here a breach of the rules of natural justice'.

On the merits of the case, therefore, the students appeared to have successfully established that they had not been treated fairly. But the exercise of discretion was still to come. First R's claim was set aside because he had 'obtained a place at the Regent Street Polytechnic in London and is no longer actively interested in returning to the University'. But P had not been so fortunate and was 'now working in a stationer's shop training for retail management'. He had expressed 'a real wish and need to return to the University'.

But, said Mr Justice Donaldson, the remedies sought

are exceptional in their nature and should not be made available to those who sleep upon their rights. Mr Partridge's complaint is that he was not allowed to resit the whole examination in June 1968, and, if successful proceed to the pass degree in the 1968-69 academic year, *yet he did not even apply to move this court until July 1968*. By such inaction, in my judgment, he forfeited whatever claims he might otherwise have had to the court's intervention. I would therefore refuse the relief sought [my italics].

Mr Justice Blain said that the court did not lightly exercise its discretion to grant the remedies sought, and they would be granted 'only where diligence is shown by an applicant in real need of the remedy'. Moreover, he had formed a view about P which was perhaps decisive. 'This court,' he said, 'should not be used for the creation of a real life counterpart to Chekhov's perpetual student.' Lord Parker C.J. had no doubt at all that the court, in the exercise of its discretion, should not give the relief claimed.

Finally, there was Mr Glynn who sunbathed, without any clothes, on the campus of Keele University, and was photographed there. The picture was sent to the vice-chancellor who wrote him a letter saying that he was fined £10 and 'excluded from residence in any residential accommodation on the university campus from today's date [1 July 1970] and for the whole of the session of 1970/1'. If the fine was not paid by 1 October, he would not be re-admitted to the University at the beginning of the next term. Mr Glynn replied at some length saying that he had had no chance to plead mitigating circumstances or to make any defence. He went abroad at the end of July before a letter from the University of 10 August gave him notice of a hearing of his appeal on 2 September. He did not return until 4 September by which time the vice-chancellor's decision had been confirmed by the appeal committee, Mr Glynn being neither present nor represented. He then sought an injunction in the courts to stop the University excluding him from residence.

The judge said:

I must next decide whether in exercising his powers in the present case the vice-chancellor complied with the requirements of natural justice. I regret that I must answer that question without hesitation in the negative. It seems to me that once one accepts that the vice-chancellor was acting in a quasi-judicial capacity, he was clearly bound to give the plaintiff an opportunity of being heard before he reached his decision on the infliction of a penalty, and if so what penalty. In fact he did not do so . . . He ought as a matter of natural justice to have sent for [the plaintiff] before he left Keele, and given him an opportunity to present his own case. With all respect to the vice-chancellor I think he failed in his duty by omitting to send for the plaintiff, and instead, writing him a letter merely announcing his decision.

But again, the discretion. The judge continued:

> I have, again after considerable hesitation, reached the conclusion that in this case I ought to exercise my discretion by not granting an injunction. I recognize that this particular discretion should be very sparingly exercised in that sense when there has been some failure in natural justice . . . There is no doubt that the *offence was one of a kind which merited a severe penalty according to any standards current even today* [my italics].

So the injunction was refused.[10]

In Bentley's case,[11] the Chief Justice said

> The vice-chancellor's authority ought to be supported for the sake of keeping peace within the University; but he must act according to law, which I do not think he has done in this case.

Those words were spoken over 250 years ago and they put side by side the two considerations which are most obvious today. Universities, polytechnics, teacher training colleges are regarded by the courts as bodies to which notions of authority and discipline are highly relevant. One case often cited is *Ex parte Fry* where a fireman refused to obey an order to clean the uniform of an officer because the order was unlawful. He was punished by his chief fire officer and asked the courts to quash that punishment on the ground that he had not had a fair hearing. Lord Goddard C.J. said

> It seems to me impossible to say that a chief officer of a force which is governed by discipline, such as a fire brigade is, in exercising disciplinary authority over a

> member of that force, acting judicially or quasi-judicially, any more than a schoolmaster is when he is exercising disciplinary powers over his pupils.

and he equated the fire brigade with the military and the police, denying to all members of those services rights of application to the courts in such circumstances. The Court of Appeal upheld the Lord Chief Justice, basing its refusal on its discretionary power to withhold the remedy.[12]

Students seem to fall near that category also, the courts being very reluctant to give a remedy to any student who seems to them to be challenging the authority of those at the administrative head of his institution. But the second limb of the statement in 1723 – that those authorities must act according to law – is now interpreted less strictly.

Thus the Privy Council generally is very reluctant to reverse decisions from the courts of overseas territories within its jurisdiction yet did so in *Fernando*'s case on insubstantial grounds. In *Ward*'s case, it is difficult to resist the impression that Lord Denning was more affected by moral conduct of which he disapproved (as was the judge in *Glynn*'s case) than by the applicability of the rules of natural justice. In *Parry*'s case the judge was clearly influenced by the student president's attitude, when the issue was more akin, in reality, to an industrial dispute to which the National Union of Students was a party.

In *Aston*'s case, the breach of the rules of natural justice was flagrant and the dispute was clearly one which had split the academic staff of the University. Yet the student lost because he was supposed to have not pursued his remedy in the courts quickly enough. Mr Justice Donaldson said :

> No explanation for this delay has been offered by either applicant but [the president of the guild of students] said that the whole matter was referred to the National Union of Students on whose advice professional legal assistance was sought, the cost being borne by that

union's student legal aid fund. He added that statements had to be taken from the students, some of whom had left the University, and that it was necessary to find out which of them wished to take legal action.

Even if there was delay between 1 November 1967 and 19 July 1968 to say that the student, dealing both with his own union and the NUS, was sleeping upon his rights, is absurd. And to link this, as did Mr Justice Blain, with references to Chekhov's perpetual student is revealing but irrelevant.

Students are not one of the more popular minorities and Her Majesty's judges in recent times seem to have shared much of the prejudice shown by other, equally senior, members of society.

TRADE UNION MEMBERS

When an individual joins a trade union he agrees to be bound by the rules of the union, present and future, contained in the rule book. The rule book prescribes penalties, such as expulsion from membership and fining, for breach of the rules. Thus there may be a power to expel a member found guilty of 'attempting to injure the union' or of 'conduct detrimental to the union'; or more specifically of failure to pay subscriptions or committing fraud on the union and other such offences. To determine such cases the rule book normally lays down a procedure and entrusts the decision to a disciplinary committee – which the courts call a domestic tribunal.

The ordinary courts over the years have developed principles to decide in what circumstances they will intervene in these proceedings. On the one hand they say that they are not and should not be courts of appeal from such domestic tribunals. Nevertheless they have insisted that a trade union member cannot be expelled from a union unless there is an express rule providing for expulsion; and where there is such a rule, there must be a

167

proper hearing and the rules of natural justice must be followed. Judicial decisions have strictly limited this power of expulsion and strictly insisted on the proper procedure. In some of the leading cases they appear to have gone further.

Thus in *Lee v. Showmen's Guild*[13] the plaintiff was fined by the union for unfair competition in relation to another member. He refused to pay the fine and, in accordance with the rules, was expelled. But the Court of Appeal set aside his expulsion on the ground that his conduct could not be said to have been unfair competition. Denning L.J. said:

> A man's right to work is just as important to him as, if not more important than, his rights of property. These courts intervene every day to protect rights of property. They must also intervene to protect the right to work.

A few years later the House of Lords decided in *Bonsor v. Musician's Union*[14] that a wrongfully expelled union member was entitled to the payment of damages from his union for the loss he had suffered, at least where there had been a breach of the rules in the rule book.

Most of the cases have arisen because of procedural defects on which the courts have been severe. In *Lawlor v. Union of Post Office Workers*[15] expulsions were set aside because there had been no proper hearing and no notification of the offences. In *Taylor v. National Union of Seamen*[16] the fatal defect was that the general secretary of the union took the chair at the meeting which heard the appeal and presented the case against the member, thus improperly doubling the roles of prosecutor and judge. In *Hiles v. Amalgamated Society of Woodworkers*[17] the court held that the appeals committee which reversed a decision in favour of the member had no jurisdiction to hear the case. In *Leary v. National Union of Vehicle Builders*[18] it was held that the member had not had a proper opportunity to meet the charge made against him. In *Edwards v. SOGAT*[19] Lord Denning held that rules which gave the union an unfettered right capriciously and arbitrarily to withdraw temporary membership without regard to the rules of natural justice were invalid. And in *Radford v. NATSOPA*,[20] the court said that had the union rules provided for automatic forfeiture of membership without the necessity for a charge and a hearing, they would have been void; but as they did require this but it was not given, the expulsion was illegal.

In *Shotton v. Hammond*[21] the court found, amongst other things, that the district committee of the union refused to approve S's election as shop steward unless he gave an undertaking to carry out the committee's instructions regardless of whether or not those instructions were authorized by the union's rules. The court in this case went so far as to issue a mandatory injunction ordering the committee to convene a meeting within fourteen days and approve S's election, and ordering the executive committee of the union to ratify this at its next monthly meeting.

From all these cases it can be seen that trade unions not infrequently act, in relation to their members, without proper regard for the rules of natural justice.

The contrast with the courts' attitude to the student cases is very great. In the latter, as we have seen, the courts seek assiduously to find some ground on which to disregard breach of the rules of natural justice. In the trade union cases they very rarely allow any such breach to be overlooked. Both groups of cases concern the right to work. Frequently both concern expulsions. The consequences of expulsion in both may be most serious to the livelihood of the individual. When there have been comparable breaches of the rules of natural justice, why is the expulsion of the union member almost always set aside and that of the student almost always upheld? It is right that the courts should protect the individual against a trade union which fails to proceed fairly against him. But why should the protection be denied to a student?

The answer to these questions lies in the general attitudes of the judiciary to which I will return in the final chapter. But in the case of students and trade unionists, it is the attitude of the judiciary to constitutional or public authority that is seen to prevail. Individual members of trade unions are seen as private citizens trying to combat large remote organizations and, moreover, organizations which are not part of the State's authority. And as we have already seen,[22] the judges have never taken kindly to trade unions in their relations with employers or the Government. So individuals are apt to be protected by the courts.

On the other hand, students are seen essentially as children and sometimes very unpleasant children – above all, as very undisciplined children. And universities and colleges are institutions of the State and so to be upheld. Both students and trade unions are seen as offering different kinds of challenge to public authority and as such to be controlled.

NOTES

1. [1951] 1 K.B. 127.
2. *Thorne v. University of London* [1966] 2 Q.B. 237.
3. *R. v. University of Cambridge* (1723) 1 Str. 237.
4. *Ridge v. Baldwin* [1964] A.C. 40.
5. *University of Ceylon v. Fernando* [1960] 1 W.L.R. 223.
6. *Ward v. Bradford Corporation* (1972) 70 L.G.R. 27.
7. [1973] 3 All E.R. 569.
8. (1972) 70 L.G.R. 576.
9. [1969] 2 Q.B. 538.
10. *Glynn v. Keele University* [1971] 1 W.L.R. 487.
11. Above, p. 151.
12. [1954] 1 W.L.R. 730.
13. [1952] 2 Q.B. 329.
14. [1956] A.C. 104.
15. [1965] 2 W.L.R. 579.

16. [1967] 1 W.L.R. 532.
17. [1968] 1 Ch. 440.
18. [1971] Ch. 34.
19. [1971] Ch. 354.
20. [1972] ICR 484.
21. *The Times* 26 October 1976.
22. Above, chapter 3.

PART THREE

Policy

*The courts hold justly a high, and I think, unequalled
pre-eminence in the respect of the world in criminal
cases, and in civil cases between man and man, no
doubt, they deserve and command the respect and
admiration of all classes of the community, but where
class issues are involved, it is impossible to pretend
that the courts command the same degree of general
confidence. On the contrary, they do not, and a very
large number of our population have been led to the
opinion that they are, unconsciously, no doubt, biassed.
[Hon. Members: 'No, no', 'Withdraw' and interruption.]*

The Secretary of State for the Home Department (Mr
W. S. Churchill) on the second reading of the Trade
Unions (No. 2) Bill, 1911 (26 H.C. Deb. col. 1022).

*The habits you are trained in, the people with whom
you mix, lead to your having a certain class of ideas
of such a nature that, when you have to deal with
other ideas, you do not give as sound and accurate
judgments as you would wish. This is one of the great
difficulties at present with Labour. Labour says
'Where are your impartial Judges? They all move in
the same circle as the employers, and they are all
educated and nursed in the same ideas as the employers.
How can a labour man or a trade unionist get impartial
justice?' It is very difficult sometimes to be sure that
you have put yourself into a thoroughly impartial
position between two disputants, one of your own class
and one not of your class.*

Lord Justice Scrutton in an address delivered to the
University of Cambridge Law Society on 18 November
1920 (1 *Cambridge Law Journal* p. 8).

I know that over 300 years ago Hobart C. J. said the 'Public policy is an unruly horse'. It has often been repeated since. So unruly is the horse, it is said (per Burrough J. in Richardson v. Mellish [1924]) *that no judge should ever try to mount it lest it run away with him. I disagree. With a good man in the saddle, the unruly horse can be kept in control. It can jump over obstacles. It can leap the fences put up by fictions and come down on the side of justice . . .*

Lord Denning M. R. in *Enderby Town Football Club v. Football Association Ltd* [1971] 1 Ch. 591.

Chapter 8: Judicial creativity

In the first chapter I referred to the importance of the creative function which judges perform both in the development of the common law and in the interpretation of statutes. All the cases in this book are examples, greater or smaller, of this function.

It was common at one time for judges to deny that they had any creative function at all or, more precisely and more positively, to assert that, in the development of the common law, all they did was to declare it. Lord Reid, one of the outstanding Law Lords of this century, has said :

> Those with a taste for fairy tales seem to have thought that in some Aladdin's cave there is hidden the Common Law in all its splendour and that on a judge's appointment there descends on him knowledge of the magic words Open Sesame. Bad decisions are given when the judge has muddled the password and the wrong door opens. But we do not believe in fairy tales any more.[1]

Nowadays, however, the argument still persists in relation to the interpretation of statutes. When a particular interpretation – for example of the Race Relations Acts – is objected to, it is common for the interpretation to be defended on the ground that all the judges can do is to apply the law as made by Parliament and not to improve it.[2]

But if the statute is open to more than one interpretation then the judges are supposed to discover, by looking at the whole of the law on the matter, including the statute itself, what was the intention of Parliament and to interpret accordingly. At this point strong disagreement may arise, even within the court itself. If the court decided that, for example, it was the intention of Parliament to exclude

Conservative clubs or dockers' clubs from the operation of the Race Relations Act 1968, some critics will say that so widespread an exception, applying to clubs with such extensive membership, is wholly contrary to the spirit and the intention of that statute. And they will go on to say that the courts are showing a restrictive attitude on a matter of social policy and politics.

On the other hand there will be those who say that the Race Relations Acts mark a serious intervention and a considerable regulation of personal relationships. Therefore, they will argue, such regulation should be kept to a minimum and Parliament should be assumed to have intended that the intervention should not be extended beyond the most explicit provision.[3]

A similar division of opinion can be seen where other forms of regulation arise – for example, in the interpretation of the legislation about the control of the use of land. Wherever private rights are regulated, whether of property or of persons, there will be those who say that the regulation should be kept to a minimum and those who say that it must not be so restricted as to weaken its application.

But the difficulty lies deeper than disagreements about the so-called 'intention of Parliament'. First, if particular judges or particular courts consistently interpret certain types of legislation either widely or narrowly they will gain the reputation either of being 'liberal', 'progressive', 'socialist' et cetera, or of being 'restrictive', reactionary', 'conservative' et cetera. Secondly, many people will simply disbelieve the judges who say that they are concerned only with ascertaining the intention of Parliament. And this disbelief is strengthened when judges express opinions, in the course of their judgments, which seem to show where their sympathies lie.

Thus Lord Denning found no difficulty in interpreting the rules of Miss Ward's college (which were made under statutory powers) so as to enable the governors to act retrospectively to her disadvantage. But he seems to have taken this view because he was sure her personal behaviour

Judicial creativity

made her unsuitable to be a teacher.[4] Similarly (though
these were common law cases) Lord Diplock drew attention to the way the law of conspiracy had developed
because 'what was proved against the defendant at the
trial was that he had done something of which the judge
and jury strongly disapproved' although he had done
nothing illegal or, if he had, was not charged with it.[5]

The attitude of the courts to the statutory rules which
give much short shrift to squatters is one of such sympathy
in words and little sympathy in interpretation of the
powers to evict. Since the judges made these rules themselves this is perhaps unsurprising but the words of
Oliver J. already quoted[6] show that he was so anxious to
do justice according to law that he protected himself and
his judicial brethren against 'the ingenuity of counsel' by
an ultra-strict interpretation. Similarly Lord Denning has
said :

It is plain that Parliament intended that the Supple-
mentary Benefit Act 1966 should be administered with
as little technicality as possible. It should not become
the happy hunting ground for lawyers. The courts
should hesitate long before interfering by certiorari with
the decision of the appeal tribunals . . . The courts
should not enter into a meticulous discussion of the
meaning of this or that word in the Act. They should
leave the tribunals to interpret the Act in a broad
reasonable way, according to the spirit and not to the
letter : especially as Parliament has given them a way
of alleviating any hardship. The courts should only
interfere when the decision of the tribunal is unreasonable in the sense that no tribunal acquainted with the
ordinary use of language could reasonably reach that
decision.[7]

How creative judges should be either in their development of the common law or their interpretation of statutes
has long been argued by the judges themselves. Lords

Diplock, Devlin and Reid are the three most distinguished recent contributors to the debate.[8]

Lord Diplock in 1965 was a Lord Justice of Appeal. He chose to talk about tax law which, he said, he was not interested in reforming – 'It no more lies within the field of morals than does a crossword puzzle.' But judicial decisions interpreting tax law affect all like cases and so the legislative content of such decisions is most obvious, especially as most cases concern transactions which Parliament had not anticipated or thought about at all. In many such cases Lord Diplock accepted that judges had to adopt a narrow, semantic and literal approach answering the question, what do the words mean? not what did the users of the words intend? But he thought the danger was that the courts also tended to apply the same criteria to statutes of a different kind which contained clear indications of general principle or policy which, in his view, ought to qualify the sense in which particular words or phrases were understood.

To Lord Diplock 'Law is about man's duty to his neighbour'. He saw the fashioning of these rules of human conduct as the proper field of judge-made law and referred with approbation to 'the bold imaginative judgments delivered by a great generation of judges between the 'sixties and the 'nineties of the last century'. This courage and imagination he found lacking in judges of the first half of this century but thought there was evidence of recent change for the better.

Seven years later, in 1972, Lord Reid wrote of 'the real difficulty' about judges making law.

Everyone agrees that impartiality is the first essential in any judge. And that means not only that he must not appear to favour either party. It also means that he must not take sides on political issues. When public opinion is sharply divided on any question – whether or not the division is on party lines – no judge ought in my view to lean to one side or the other if that can

178

possibly be avoided. But sometimes we get a case where that is very difficult to avoid. Then I think we must play safe. We must decide the case on the preponderance of existing authority.

This caution extended even to those cases where there was 'some freedom to go in one or other direction'. 'We should,' continued Lord Reid, 'have regard to common sense, legal principle and public policy in that order' and he made it clear that the first two criteria were unlikely to leave much scope for the application of the third.

Lord Devlin's position was more elaborate but in the end closer to Lord Reid's than to Lord Diplock's. He distinguished 'activist' from 'dynamic' law-making. The first meant keeping pace with change in the consensus; the second meant generating change in the consensus. And he said that the consensus in a community consisted of those ideas which its members as a whole liked or, if they disliked, would submit to. So he argued that the law had been used cautiously in the field of race relations with some success; but not so cautiously in the field of industrial relations without success. For Lord Devlin the social service which judges rendered was the removal of a sense of injustice and for this both impartiality and the appearance of impartiality were essential. Lord Devlin is clear that the judge should never be a dynamic law-maker.

The discussion about how creative judges should be, how far the approach to statutes should be literal and semantic, or seeking 'the intention' of Parliament, and other variants on the same theme, has been continuing for many years. Yet it has been and is a somewhat unreal discussion. While in certain circumstances and on some specific issues particular judges can be shown, from the record of their decisions, to belong more to the creative or more to the conservative school, it is very doubtful whether either tendency follows from one or other general judicial position. Lord Diplock is not regarded as a more creative judge than was Lord Reid, and Lord Devlin was thought of by some as a more creative judge than either.[9]

All this leads to the conclusion that, as one might expect, judges like the rest of us are not all of a piece, that they are liable to be swayed by emotional prejudices, that their 'inarticulate major premises' are strong and not only inarticulated but sometimes unknown to themselves. The judges seldom give the impression of strong silent men wedded only to a sanctified impartiality. They frequently appear – and speak – as men with weighty, even passionate, views of the nature of society and the content of law and of their partial responsibility for its future development.

Individualistic strains could, of course, exist alongside a consistent attitude to creativity or its opposite. What is lacking however is any clear and consistent relationship between the general pronouncement of judges on this matter of creativity and the way they conduct themselves in court. Lord Simonds was Lord Chancellor in 1951-4 and is often quoted as the exemplar of the conservative view. Thus in one case he said that he would not 'easily be led by an undiscerning zeal for some abstract kind of justice or ignore our first duty, which is established for us by Act of Parliament or the binding authority of precedent'.[10] Yet it was he who in the previous year had discovered that there was an offence known to the common law of conspiracy to corrupt public morals, a view which caused no little surprise in legal and political circles.[11]

For a time Lord Simonds and Lord Denning carried on a public dispute, the latter making a strong plea for the creative function. Lord Denning, like Lord Simonds, is a reminder that creativity is neither good nor bad but that thinking makes it so. When he supported the action of the college governors in changing the rules of discipline to enable them to dismiss the woman student who was found to have a man in her room, he was certainly acting 'creatively'.[12] When he sought to protect the rights of demonstrators to protest outside the offices of the estate

agents in *Hubbard v. Pitt* he was refusing to be bound by
an earlier procedural decision which his colleagues on
the bench thought binding on them. And he did so on
strong liberal principles. The view taken by Lord Denning
can be seen as either creative (refusing to be bound by
the earlier decision) or conservative (maintaining the traditional rights of individuals to 'free speech', as he put it).

I am arguing that the public position adopted by judges
in the controversy about creativity is not consistently reflected in their judgments and that more important are
their reactions to the moral, political and social issues in
the cases that come before them.

The law reports abound with references to the duty of
the courts to abide by the provisions of Acts of Parliament. But that does not help in deciding how to deal with
ambiguities or obscurities. In *Chandler v. D.P.P.*[13] Lord
Reid said:

> Of course we are bound by the words which Parliament
> has used in the Act. If those words necessarily lead to
> that conclusion then it is no answer that it is incon-
> ceivable that Parliament can have so intended. The
> remedy is to amend the Act. But we must be clear that
> the words of the Act are not reasonably capable of any
> other interpretation.

The 'conclusion' referred to was that Parliament in
passing the Official Secrets Act in 1911 intended that a
person who deliberately interfered with vital dispositions
of the armed forces should be entitled to submit to a jury
that Government policy was wrong and that what he did
was really in the best interests of the country. Lord Reid
continued:

> The question whether it is beneficial to use the armed
> forces in a particular way or prejudicial to interfere
> with that use would be a political question – a question
> of opinion on which anyone actively interested in

politics, including jurymen, might consider his own opinion as good as that of anyone else. Our criminal system is not devised to deal with issues of that kind. The question therefore is whether the Act can reasonably be read in such a way as to avoid the raising of such issues.

Lord Reid concluded that it could be read 'in such a way' and that the submissions about Government policy were rightly excluded.

The problem in *Charter* (the Conservative club case) and the *Dockers' Labour Club* case[14] was where to draw the line between 'public' and 'private' in interpreting the Race Relations Act of 1968. In both cases Lord Reid extended the notion of what was private far beyond the domestic sphere. As he said in *Charter*:

I would infer from the Act as a whole that the legislature thought all discrimination on racial grounds deplorable but thought it unwise or unpracticable to attempt to apply legal sanctions in situations of a purely private character.

The three members of the Court of Appeal and one member of the House of Lords disagreed with Lord Reid and with the majority in the Lords. It is difficult to believe that the judges in these cases did not consider the effect their views would have on race relations. It is difficult to believe that such consideration would be regarded as improper by the ordinary layman. It was, after all, what the Act of Parliament was concerned with.

Similarly, are we expected to assume that the House of Lords did not take into account or were ignorant of the effect of their decision in *Rookes v. Barnard*?[15] The realities were referred to by Lord Devlin. He said:

But there is one argument, or at least one consideration, that remains to be noticed. It is that the strike weapon is now so generally sanctioned that it cannot really be regarded as an unlawful weapon of intimidation; and so there must be something wrong with a conclusion that treats it as such. This thought plainly influenced quite strongly the judgments in the Court of Appeal . . . I see the force of this consideration. But your Lordships can, in my opinion, give effect to it only if you are prepared either to hobble the common law in all classes of disputes lest its range is too wide to suit industrial disputes or to give the statute a wider scope than it was ever intended to have.

The Court of Appeal had held that the tort of intimidation did not include a threat to break a contract. The Law Lords, including Lords Devlin and Reid, held that it did. And so a crucial section of the Act of 1906 received an interpretation nearly 60 years later which challenged the right to strike and had to be corrected by another statute.[16] Lord Devlin warned their Lordships of the dangers of the courts interfering in 'matters of policy' in this branch of the law although this was certainly the consequence of their decision. Again, creativity or its opposite is not the issue.

One group of decisions well illustrates the difficulties. We have seen that in *Shaw v. D.P.P.* (1961)[17] the House of Lords invented a new crime called 'conspiracy to corrupt public morals'. This was certainly a creative decision and one which Lord Reid dissented from in that case. He said:

Notoriously, there are wide differences of opinion today as to how far the law ought to punish immoral acts which are not done in the face of the public . . . Parliament is the proper place, and I am firmly of opinion the only proper place, to settle that. When there is sufficient support from public opinion, Parliament does not hesitate to intervene. Where Parliament fears to tread it is not for the courts to rush in.

Nine years later the House of Lords in a judgment delivered by Lord Diplock and concurred in by the other Law Lords (including Lord Reid) allowed the appeal of Mr Bhagwan[18] who had been convicted of a conspiracy to evade immigration control although he had not committed any wrong. The House of Lords could certainly have followed the lead given in *Shaw*'s case – Lords Morris and Hodson sat in both cases – but preferred to distinguish it and Lord Diplock used words which seemed to seek to diminish the importance of *Shaw*'s case.

Then in 1972 came the decision in *Knuller*[19] (the *IT* case). The Court of Appeal followed *Shaw*'s case and upheld the convictions of conspiracy to corrupt public morals. The House of Lords (Lord Diplock dissenting) upheld the Court of Appeal on this count. Lords Morris and Kilbrandon did so on the ground that *Shaw*'s case was rightly decided. Lord Reid (with Lords Morris and Simon) did so on the ground that even if it were wrongly decided it must stand until it was altered by Parliament.

Lord Reid said:

I dissented in Shaw's case. On reconsideration I still think that the decision was wrong . . . But I think that however wrong or anomalous the decision may be it must stand and apply to cases reasonably analogous unless or until it is altered by Parliament . . . Parliament alone is the proper authority to change the law with regard to the punishment of immoral acts.

It is a logical but curious position to adopt. Lord Reid said in *Shaw*'s case that the House of Lords should not there act creatively but his advice was not regarded. But when the opportunity arose in *Knuller* to reverse the decision in *Shaw*'s case, Lord Reid refused to do so because that also would be to act creatively in an area where the courts should not do so.

Lord Diplock had no such qualms. He said:

My Lords, this appeal raises two questions of out-standing importance . . . The first is: whether the decision of the majority of this House in *Shaw*'s case upon the count which charged a conspiracy to corrupt public morals was right. I think that it was wrong. The second is: ought it to be followed even if it was wrong. I think that it should not.

Since 1966, the House of Lords has considered itself not bound by its own decisions.[20] But it is reluctant to overrule them as this, it is argued, would introduce more uncertainty into the law. As Lord Reid said elsewhere:

I would venture the opinion that the typical case for reconsidering an old decision is where some broad issue is involved, and that it should only be in rare cases that we should reconsider questions of construction of statutes or other documents. In very many cases it cannot be said positively that one construction is right and the other wrong . . . Much may depend on one's approach. *If more attention is paid to meticulous exam-ination of the language used in the statute the result may be different from that reached by paying more attention to the apparent object of the statute so as to adopt that meaning of the words under consideration which best accord with it.*[21]

The words I have emphasized indicate how the differ-ences between the more literal and the more creative approaches may lead to different conclusions.

NOTES

1. *The Judge as Law Maker* in 12 J.S.P.T.L. 22 (1972).
2. See, for example, Lord Hailsham in a letter to *The Times* on 25 October 1974.
3. Cp. Lord Diplock in the *Dockers' Club* case; p. 89 above.

4. See above, pp. 154-7.
5. See above, p. 147.
6. See above, pp. 120-1.
7. *Ex parte Moore* [1975] 1 W.L.R. 624.
8. Lord Reid on *The Judge as Law Maker* (1972). (See above,). 175 note 1); Lord Devlin on *Judges and Lawmakers* in 39 *4.L.R.* 1 (1976); Lord Diplock on *The Courts as Legislators* Holdsworth Club, University of Birmingham 1965).
9. Lord Devlin retired from the bench in 1964 at the age of 58.
10. *Scruttons Ltd v. Midland Silicones* [1962] A.C. 446.
11. *Shaw v. D.P.P.* (see above, pp. 137-8).
12. See above, pp. 154-7.
13. [1962] 3 W.L.R. 694; see above pp. 141-2.
14. See above, p. 89.
15. See above, pp. 67-8.
16. Trades Disputes Act 1965.
17. See above, pp. 137-8.
18. See above, p. 94.
19. See above, pp. 139-40.
20. See [1966] 1 W.L.R. 1234.
21. *Jones v. Secretary of State* [1972] 1 All E.R. 145.

Chapter 9: The political role

In the traditional view, the function of the judiciary[1] is to decide disputes in accordance with the law and with impartiality. The law is thought of as an established body of principles which prescribes rights and duties. Impartiality means not merely an absence of personal bias or prejudice in the judge but also the exclusion of 'irrelevant' considerations such as his political or religious views. Individual litigants expect to be heard fairly and fully and to receive justice. Essentially, this view rests on an assumption of judicial 'neutrality'.

This neutrality is regarded as more than impartiality between the parties. It means, also, that the judge should not advert to matters which go beyond those necessary for decision in the case before him. On this view the judge is not to take into account any consequences which might flow from his decision and which are wider than the direct interests of the parties. He must act like a political, economic, and social eunuch, and have no interest in the world outside his court when he comes to judgment.

Where the issues are simple and the dispute limited to the interests of the two parties, the judge may fulfil his traditional function. Divorce, the meaning of a contract between businessmen, a personal claim for injury sustained in a road accident, the buying and selling of a house – for these the traditional view often suffices. But less simple issues can easily emerge. If there are children of the marriage which is to be dissolved, if the purpose of the contract is contrary to public policy, if the accident was caused by dangerous driving, if the seller is a bankrupt, then other persons and even the State itself may be involved. And their interests may have to be taken into account.

Moreover, these are all civil cases. But if the proceedings are for alleged crimes, then the State is almost always directly concerned and considerations again arise which go beyond the individuals themselves.

A more sophisticated version of this traditional view sees the judiciary as one of the principal organs of a democratic society without whom government could be carried on only with great difficulty. The essence of their function is the maintenance of law and order and the judges are seen as a mediating influence. Democracy requires that some group of persons acts as an arbiter not only between individuals but also between Governmental power and the individual. In criminal matters this Governmental power will be exercised through the police to bring a wrongdoer before the court. It will ensure that the order of the court is enforced, that prisons are provided, that fines are paid. But there must be some body, other than the Government, which hears the case, makes the decision, and decides the sentence. By this means the daily use, by the Government and its agencies, of *force* is legitimated and so made acceptable to society at large.

Judges then, in this view, are an essential part of government but exist to operate as a part of democratic organization. They take their place alongside the other two great institutions of the Executive and Parliament, more passive than they, but indispensable. No doubt there is something of a dilemma in the judiciary's position as both upholders of law and order and protectors of the individual against a powerful Executive. But this is explained in terms of checks and balances or countervailing power and so what might be an inherent contradiction dissolves in a cloud of words which nevertheless, be it noted, defines the function of the judiciary in *political* terms.

In these terms, therefore, the judiciary may come into conflict with the Government (the Executive) of the day. Formally, this conflict can arise only where the Government acts 'illegally'. But it is the judges who, particularly in their creative and interpretative function, determine whether Governments or their agents have so acted. Thus they set limits to the discretionary powers of Governments and to the rights of individuals, especially when these two forces conflict. Where and how they set those limits has been the theme of this book.

Governments have extensive powers and, with adequate Parliamentary majorities, can add to them without too much difficulty. This being so, it is well that judges should be willing to ensure that Governmental bodies do not seek to act beyond those powers. And no doubt the existence of the courts and of opportunities to bring before them dubious exercises of Governmental power is some deterrent to any public servants who may be inclined to stretch their powers beyond legal limits. So also where statutes lay down procedures to be followed before powers are exercised, the courts should insist that those procedures are followed and may even add their own gloss to ensure that Governmental bodies do not act unfairly or in bad faith. How far beyond those elementary propositions of principle the judges should go, how far they should exercise their own wide powers further to control Governmental activity, is the crucial political question.

THE MYTH OF NEUTRALITY

I have said that, traditionally, impartiality is thought of as part of a wider, judicial neutrality. Judges are seen essentially as arbiters in conflicts – whether between individuals or between individuals and the State – and as having no position of their own, no policy even in the widest sense of that word.

In denying such neutrality, I am not concerned merely to argue that judges, like other people, have their own personal political convictions and, with more or less enthusiasm, privately support one or other of the political parties and may vote accordingly. That, no doubt, is true but political partisanship in that sense is not important.

What matters is the function they perform and the role they perceive themselves as fulfilling in the political structure.

Neither impartiality nor independence necessarily involves neutrality. Judges are part of the machinery of authority within the State and as such cannot avoid the making of political decisions. What is important is to know the bases on which these decisions are made.

Lord Devlin put this most clearly when he wrote immediately after the industrial dispute of 1972 and when the five dockers had just been released from prison (see above, p. 72). He made a distinction between consensus and non-consensus law, by consensus meaning a result which people generally were 'prepared to put up with'. 'Most law,' said Lord Devlin, 'is in fact based on this sort of consensus. It is what gives the law its stability and saves it from change after every swing of the pendulum.' The Industrial Relations Act 1971, continued Lord Devlin, was not based on consensus and he asked what was the position of the courts to such law. Lord Devlin then said:

> The question would not need to be asked if in Britain the role of the courts was in accordance with theory. In theory the judiciary is the neutral force between Government and the governed. The judge interprets and applies the law without favour to either and its application in a particular case is embodied in an order which is passed to the executive to enforce. It is not the judge's personal order; it is substantially the product of the law and only marginally of the judicial mind. If its enforcement is resisted or evaded, the judge is no more concerned than if he were an arbitrator.
>
> British judges have never practised such detachment. The reason may lie in their origin as servants of the Crown or perhaps in the fact that for a long time the law they administered was what they had made themselves. A mixture of the two has left the High Court with the power to enforce its orders in civil cases by

treating disobedience as contempt itself.

In the criminal law the judges regard themselves as at least as much concerned as the executive with the preservation of law and order. Then there is what can best be described as the expatiatory power. Whereas under most systems the judgment is formal, brief and to the legal point, the British judge may expatiate on what he is doing and why he is doing it and its consequences; and because of his prestige he is listened to.

These high powers make the British judiciary more than just a neutral arbitral force. On the whole their wise and cautious deployment has enabled the judiciary to use its reputation for impartiality and independence for the public good. But it is imperative that the high powers should not be used except in support of consensus law. If the judges are to do more than decide what the law means, if they are also to speak for it, their voice must be the voice of the community; it must never be taken for the voice of the Government or the voice of the majority.

So, he argued, non-consensus law should not be enforceable by the courts and he criticized the way the Industrial Relations Act involved the courts in making orders for the enforcement of strike ballots and cooling-off orders. 'The prestige of the judiciary,' concluded Lord Devlin, 'their reputation for stark impartiality to be kept up in appearance as well as in fact, is not at the disposal of any Government: it is an asset that belongs to the whole nation.'[2]

The distinction drawn between consensus and non-consensus law is not easy to sustain. Every Government passes a number of politically controversial statutes – commonly about ten in each session – which contain much that is objected to by a large section of the electorate. Tax provisions, nationalization, housing finance, pay beds, industrial relations, comprehensive schooling, race relations, all these are obvious recent examples. If Lord Devlin means to limit non-consensus legislation only to those measures which people generally are not 'prepared to put up with' then his list will be very short indeed. If he means to extend it to include those major areas of controversy just exemplified then the list will be much longer. Is he saying that the enforcement procedures of the courts should not be used where, for example, council tenants refuse to pay rents, or councillors refuse to pay sums surcharged on them after an auditor's examination, or a member of the National Front refuses to remove a sign from his property which is in breach of the Race Relations Act, or a parent keeps his child away from a comprehensive school, or Welsh students disrupt court proceedings?

Surely Lord Devlin is trying to have it both ways. If the judiciary is more than 'a neutral arbitral force' – and I agree that it is – then it is most obviously so in controversial matters where its 'deployment' of power is highlighted. When the public interest is involved, judges become active and cannot suddenly become coy about enforcing laws – if necessary by their own procedures – which they believe to be politically controversial. Judges are in the business of upholding the law and that means they are part of the machinery for enforcing party political law as much as other 'consensus' legislation. Moreover Lord Devlin is wrong if he believes that trade union distrust of the judiciary flows from the fact that the enforcement of the order for committal to prison of the dockers was effected by court officials rather than by other public servants. It was the order of the court that mattered not the method of its enforcement.

Nevertheless, when all this is said, the importance of Lord Devlin's analysis rests in his denial of the neutrality of the judiciary in matters like the criminal law and, I would add, inevitably whenever judges set limits, as they frequently do, to Governmental powers and individual rights in circumstances where statutes and common law give guidance which is inadequate or imprecise.

THE PUBLIC INTEREST AND ITS APPLICATION

At this point the traditional views become inadequate as descriptions of what judges do. The judges determine (where doubts arise) the limits of Governmental powers and of individual rights. But as the law has not provided them with full indications of where those limits are to be drawn, they must have regard to some concept on which they can base their judgments.

The higher judiciary comprises some hundred persons, but the truly effective number of policy-makers in the Divisional Court, the Court of Appeal and the House of Lords is fewer than thirty. *These judges have by their education and training and the pursuit of their profession as barristers, acquired a strikingly homogeneous collection of attitudes, beliefs and principles, which to them represents the public interest.* They do not always express it as such. But it is the lodestar by which they navigate.

I use 'the public interest' because that is the phrase most used by the judges themselves when they choose to be explicit. Sometimes they speak of 'the interests of the State' but this carries a somewhat narrower meaning and suggests either the interests of the United Kingdom internationally or the interests of good government. 'The national interest' is synonymous, in judicial usage, with State interests. I take 'the public interest' to embrace both these other phrases but also to include the interest of the people at large, especially when contrasted with the interests of sections of the people.

What is or is not in the public interest is a political question which admits of a great variety of answers. On important issues, especially where there are only two or three possible alternative courses of action, personal opinions easily become part of group opinions. Indeed, as conventional rhetoric, political parties always claim that their policies, and not those of their opponents, best serve the public interest. Another truism is that I will be inclined to identify my interests with those of the public.

If I am chairman of General Motors I will be inclined to think that what is good for General Motors is good for the nation. But my own interests, as I see them, will not be limited to my obvious economic interests. They may include, for instance, the continuing stability of the society in which I live, or the continuance of those surrounding circumstances which may give my life meaning.

Clearly then, what the Government proposes to do may, or may not, in my opinion, promote the public interest. To accuse the Government of not acting in the public interest is the oldest political criticism.

Judges in the United Kingdom are not beholden politically to the Government of the day. And they have longer professional lives than most Ministers. They, like civil servants, see Governments come like water and go with the wind. They owe no loyalty to Ministers, not even that temporary loyalty which civil servants owe. Coke said that Bracton said that the King ought to be under no man but under God and the law.[3] Judges are also lions under the throne but that seat is occupied in their eyes not by the Prime Minister but by the law and by their conception of the public interest. It is to that law and to that conception that they owe allegiance. In that lies their strength and their weakness, their value and their threat.

By allegiance to 'the law' judges mean the whole body of law much of which has its origins in the judge-made common law. 'The law' also means the rule of law and here the allegiance is to the philosophical ideal that we should be ruled by laws and not by men. If that means that power should not be exercised arbitrarily or on the whim of rulers and their officials but should be dependent on and flow from properly constituted authority and from rules written down and approved by some form of representative assembly, it is an admirable and necessary, if partial, safeguard against tyranny. The proposition can hardly be taken further because, in modern industrial society, it is impossible to avoid vesting considerable discretionary power in public officials if only because laws cannot be adequately framed to cover every eventuality.

The judicial conception of the public interest, seen in the cases discussed in this book, is threefold. It concerns, first, the interests of the State (including its moral welfare) and the preservation of law and order, broadly interpreted; secondly, the protection of property rights; and thirdly the promotion of certain political views normally associated with the Conservative party.

First, then, the interests of the State, as the basis of judicial law-making, are most obvious in cases where the country is seen as being in an emergency of national dimensions. The civil liberty cases like *Liversidge v. Anderson, Greene, Halliday* and others (see above, pp. 79-81) are examples, and it is significant, that the so-called libertarian principles which are said to lie behind habeas corpus and other such remedies have seldom proved strong enough to prevail over the interests of the State in these circumstances – as Mr Soblen and Mr Hosenball discovered (see above, pp. 95, 81).

But the interests of the State, or the national interests, are invoked more widely as the basis for judicial policies. The exercise of judicial legerdemain which sprang the five dockers from prison in 1972 was certainly motivated by the imminence of a probable general strike (see above, p. 72). So also the national interest in the administration of justice was appealed to – unconvincingly – by the judges when they decided to stifle further discussion by the *Sunday Times* of the thalidomide scandal (see above, pp. 98-9).

The power of the Crown to claim that documents ought not, in the public interest, to be disclosed, conflicts directly with the political claim that the public has a right to know unless strong evidence is adduced to the contrary. In *Conway v. Rimmer* (see above, p. 102) the House of Lords shifted their interpretation of where the public interest lay a little towards the interest of the public. But Lord Reid swept aside in the grand bureaucratic manner a few democratic rights when he said that the most important reason for preserving secrecy for

Government documents was that their disclosure might 'create or fan ill-informed or captious public or political criticism' from those 'without adequate knowledge of the background and perhaps with some axe to grind' (see above, p. 103). On the other hand, the Lord Chief Justice in the Crossman diaries case (see above, p. 100) may have introduced his judicial colleagues to new and dangerous opportunities for the exercise of their conception of the nature and extent of the public interest and have established a new legal principle of confidentiality under which the views of Ministers and former Ministers could be suppressed without resort to the Official Secrets Act. But for that we must wait and see.

The public interest expressly informs the attitude of the courts to questions of moral behaviour. Lord Denning's 'She would never make a teacher. No parent would willingly entrust their child to her care' was no doubt a trivial, though revealing, comment (see above, p. 157). But the great periods of the rhetoric of Viscount Simonds, creating a new crime of conspiracy to corrupt public morals, when he claimed that the courts had the power 'to enforce the supreme and fundamental purpose of the law, to conserve not only the safety and order but also the moral welfare of the State' (see above, p. 137) were not trivial at all.

As Lord Devlin has said, in the passage already quoted (see above, p. 191), 'the judges regard themselves as at least as much concerned as the executive with the preservation of law and order'. One of the greatest political myths is that the courts in this country are alert to protect the individual against the power of the State. Sometimes, it is true, they will intervene to help the weakest, as some of the immigration cases show. But minority groups, especially if they demonstrate or protest in ways which cause difficulty or embarrassment, are not likely to find that the courts support their claims to free speech or free assembly. The judges see themselves as occupying key positions in the struggle to enforce the law, and are always conscious of the dangers which they believe will follow if they do not support the powers of the police. But the preservation of law and order is absurdly stretched when it is made to protect university officials whose 'authority is deliberately flouted by an insubordinate student' (see above, p. 161).

The student cases indeed are excellent examples of the judicial obsession with, as they see it, the necessity to protect and preserve the structures of constitutional authority without undue concern for the rights of those who wish to challenge that authority. Student protest is seen as essentially a problem of law and order.

The judicial attitude has been almost wholly condemnatory, seemingly based on the assumption that if students oppose university or college authorities they must be acting unreasonably. Here the view of the courts seems to have been based, fairly simply, on the public interest in maintaining 'discipline' regarding adult educational institutions rather as if they were public boarding schools.

Demonstrations, if properly organized and controlled by the police, are acceptable by the judiciary as being within the framework of law and order. But individual demonstrators are always likely to be viewed with considerable disfavour by the courts. Although very different in kind, two of the most repressive decisions handed down in recent years were those in *Kamara* (see above, p. 142) and in *Hubbard v. Pitt* (see above, p. 145). Lord Hailsham's extension of the criminal law to cover peaceful sit-ins and occupations as a method of demonstration in the first of these cases, and the Court of Appeal's finding for the estate agents against peaceful demonstrators in the second, mark once more the willingness of the judiciary to extend the rather special judicial conception of where the public interest lies into the areas of political controversy.

In perhaps the most important area of all, that of police powers (see above, p. 83), the judges have left largely unfulfilled their self-styled role as protectors of the individual. The practice of the police in relation to questioning, search and seizure, access to lawyers, the obtaining of confessions, the conduct of identification parades, has frequently, in recent years, stretched far beyond their powers and infringed not only the spirit of the law but its letter also. Suspects have been held for long periods of time 'helping the police with their enquiries' and solicitors have been positively prevented by the police from seeing their clients. These practices have been generally supported by the judiciary. When on 2 July 1976 Lord Justice Lawton in the Court of Appeal warned customs and police officers against detaining people to help with enquiries and refusing solicitors access to clients, as happened in the case before him, the press treated his statement as remarkable and one legal journalist went so far as to say that the Lord Justice had 'blown the gaffe'.[4] The reaction was more revealing than the statement.

The second aspect of the public interest, as seen by the judges, is the protection of private property. Here the tradition stems from the common law so much of which arose specifically for the purpose of settling disputes relating to land and settlements. In public law, the disputes arise because of the power of the State to control the use of land, to acquire land for public purposes or for slum clearance, or in other ways (where the notion of property extends to rights in interests other than land) to limit the activities of personal owners. We have seen (above, pp. 107-21) how, apart from a brief period during and after the Second World War, the courts have continuously intervened to limit and curtail the powers of Governments to interfere with property rights and that they have been far more assiduous in this than in the protection of civil rights or liberties.

Squatters almost inevitably engage the ingenuity of judges to ensure that the law is kept as tight as possible with no loopholes. They are trespassers on property, they are often young, they may be uncivil in their approach to the authorities, they are generally poor and they demonstrate (especially when, as often, they are families with young children) the inability of society to deal with the problems caused by housing shortages (see above, p. 116).

Not only the attitude but the very function of the judiciary in modern society are exemplified and emphasized by the difference in the protection of property rights and of personal human rights. Indeed 'rights' itself has two separate meanings in this content. Property rights are vested in individuals by the operation of the law. Contracts, leases, trusts, wills and settlements are all ways of creating and transferring these rights in law. And the protection of these rights is the primary purpose of a legal system. The law protects legal rights as they are. Its function, and that of the judiciary, is to maintain the existing state of affairs.

Personal – or human – rights are not vested rights but claims. Even when they are presently enjoyed to some extent they have to be continuously insisted on and continuously fought for. Any carelessness in the protection of freedom leads directly to their erosion. Moreover, the enlargement of my freedom, my liberties, means the diminution of power, to however small an extent, enjoyed by some other person or, more likely, some official or institution. When, therefore, the judiciary is asked to defend such personal rights, it is being asked not to protect but to assert, not to strengthen institutions but to weaken them. And this is something which judges are reluctant to do for it is alien to their principal function which is not the enlargement of liberty, but the preservation of legally vested rights.

The attitude of the courts to trade union members who incur the displeasure of union officials is, as we have seen, one of considerable sympathy. When it can be shown that the officials have acted unfairly or improperly, this sympathy is well-placed for it is a most serious matter to deprive a man of his livelihood. Yet the same sympathy is not extended to the same degree to those who claim that their companies have unjustly dismissed them. And the suspicion arises that the courts in protecting the individual trade unionist are motivated more by their dislike of organized trade unions than by their wish to advance the personal rights of individuals.

The third aspect of the public interest is, I have suggested, the promotion of certain political, conservative views. First there are the trade union cases. We have seen (see above, p. 57) that the prevailing view of the senior judiciary in the late nineteenth and early twentieth centuries was, in conflict with much of the Governmental view of the time, that the growing power of the trade unions should be strictly controlled by law. The judges were seeking to undo some of the effects of earlier legislation and Lord Halsbury, as Lord Chancellor, led them to some success in this attempt. When, over half a century later, the judges and the unions once more came into conflict, the Government had adopted the judicial view which was shown in the picketing cases, *Rookes v. Barnard,* and the culmination in *Heaton's* case and the imprisonment by the NIRC of the five dockers (see above, pp. 70-7). Nor is the view unpopular. But when the economic consequences of the continued detention of the dockers and the threat of a general strike became clear, then what was in 'the public interest' was seen to have changed dramatically, and the dockers were released. The President of the NIRC imprisoned the dockers expressly in defence of the rule of law when to ignore their challenge would be to 'imperil all law and order', on which 'our whole way of life' was based. A few days later he released them – also, expressly, in defence of the rule of law – having been provided by the House of Lords with a flimsy justification for so doing (see above, p. 72).

So the National Industrial Relations Court in 1972 forced the judiciary to take up a position on the Government's side of industrial disputes which divided the country (see above, p. 76). But, especially here, the distinction must be observed between the interests of the Government of the day and the judiciary's view of the public interest.

Certainly, the two interests coincided for the judges enabled the Government to escape from a situation which would probably have brought it down and would have presented the trade union movement with a considerable political victory. The judges, we may assume, were not concerned to save that particular Conservative Government. They were concerned, however, both to preserve the authority of Governments and to avoid economic chaos. That was where they saw the public interest to lie. The price they paid was the increase in distrust between themselves and the trade union movement. So they may have mistaken the public interest. But that is a political comment about a political choice.

The approach of the courts to the Race Relations Acts, as shown in the decisions in Zesko and the club cases particularly, proceeds on the basis that this legislation is primarily an interference with the rights of individuals to discriminate and that the public interest is best served by restricting the impact of that legislation as far as possible (see above, p. 87). Despite the natural conservatism of the House of Lords, this does seem to be a more than usually restrictive attitude. The alternative interpretation of the legislation was so clearly available to their Lordships that it is impossible to avoid the conclusion that theirs was a deliberate policy decision.

Lord Diplock perhaps gives the key when he speaks of the Race Relations Act 'however admirable its motive' as restricting liberty. The idea of intervening by legislation in this way with the freedom 'enjoyed at common law to differentiate between one person and another' was clearly offensive to him, as it is indeed to many.

The attitude of the judiciary to immigrants has on occasion been rather more protective in an area of official action which is often harshly administered and where the consequence of refusal to admit is severe, whether necessary or not. But most recently this judicial mitigation of official action seems to have been abandoned – if the Lords' decision in *Suthendran* is an indication. Certainly, that decision was not unanimous and the applicant can be accounted unfortunate in his court. But it is, at best, a valuable reminder that the Law Lords, or some of them, are not inclined to interpret such legislation in the immigrant's favour.

The judicial view of the public interest shown in the more recent decisions limiting Ministerial discretion shows the dislike which judges have for legislation or for administrative activity which affects property rights. In *Padfield, Anisminic*, the TV licence case, and *Laker*, the judges upheld the private citizen against the Government. However when a trade union challenged Ministerial power in *Aslef No. 2* (see above, p. 124), the Minister was upheld, suggesting once again that judges operate on the premise that other things being equal or unequal, trade unions (like students) shall lose. Whether there are more direct political explanations for these decisions is considered below.

CONCLUSION

In suggesting that the judges look to a view of the public interest to inform their attitude to the controversial matters of law and order, of political and economic conflict, of sexual and social *mores*, of personal liberty and property rights, of protest, of governmental confidentiality, of students and squatters, of race relations, of immigration and the rest, I mean to absolve them of a conscious and deliberate intention to pursue their own interests or the interests of their class. I believe that in these matters and within the considerable area of decision-making open to them they look to what they regard as the interest of the whole society. However, we are left to consider why it is that their view of that public interest is what it is.

It is common to speak of the judiciary as part of the system of checks and balances which contains and constrains the power of the Government; or as one of the three principal institutions of the State, each of which acts to limit the powers of the other two. The image has a pleasing and mechanistic appearance suggesting some objective hidden hand which holds the constitution in perpetual equilibrium. The extent to which the image reflects reality is less obvious.

If we limit our examination to the working of the three institutions – Parliament, the Government, and the Judiciary – in their relationships with each other, then it is clear that each of these groups influences the way in which the others act. And it is clear, in particular, that the judiciary may oppose the Government to the extent of declaring its actions invalid or requiring it to pay compensation or even subjecting one of its members or servants to penalties.

If however we look more broadly and more widely we see that this judicial activity of opposing Governments is a deviance from the norm, an aberration, which occurs most infrequently and in very special circumstances. The judiciary is not placed constitutionally in opposition to the Government but, in the overwhelming mass of circumstances, alongside it.

In our society, as in others, political power, the power of government, is exercised by a relatively small number of people. Ministers are most obviously of that number, as are senior civil servants, chairmen of nationalized industries, the chairmen and chief officers of the largest local authorities. Amongst those who are not members of State institutions should be added a few industrialists and a few trade union leaders. And the leading members of Her Majesty's Opposition are also, from time to time, a part of the decision-making process at this highest level. The whole group numbers a few hundred people.

The rest are outside. Some may be influential as advisors. Others may be very important as professional men and women. But they, along with the population at large, remain outside the governing group. Of course there are many organizations which exercise many different kinds of power within their own sphere. In this narrow sense, we live in a pluralist society. But the political power of governing the country is oligarchic, exercised by a few.

The senior judges are undeniably amongst those few. The importance of their task, their influence on behaviour, the extent of their powers, the status they enjoy, the extra-judicial uses to which they are put, the circles they move in, the background from which they come, their habits of mind, and the way in which they are regarded by other members of the group confirm beyond question their place within the governing group. And, like other members of the group, they show themselves alert to protect the social order from threats to its stability or to the existing distribution of political and economic power.

I have said that judges look to what they regard as the interests of the whole society. That, in itself, makes political assumptions of some magnitude. It has long been argued that the concept of the whole society suggests a homogeneity of interest amongst the different classes within that society which is false. And that this concept is used to persuade the governed that not the Government but 'the State' is the highest organization and transcends conflicts in society. It is a short step to say that it is the State which makes the laws, thus enabling those in political power to promote their own interests in the name of the whole abstracted society.

In this analysis also, the judges are seen as an integral part of the government of the State. Rules are made by the Government or, through the common law, by the judiciary. These rules are 'the law' and that phrase gives them a supra-political respectability. The rules are what they are because of the nature of the society, because of its cultural and particularly its economic ordering. The Government is the political manifestation of the economic forces and the judiciary also subserves those forces. In modern Marxist terms:

From this standpoint the law is, perhaps more clearly than any other cultural or institutional artifact, by definition a part of a 'superstructure' adapting itself to the necessities of an infra-structure of productive forces and productive relations. As such it is clearly an instrument of the *de facto* ruling class: it both defines these rulers' claims upon resources and labour-power – it says what shall be property and what shall be crime – and it mediates class relations with a set of appropriate rules and sanctions, all of which, ultimately, confirm and consolidate class power. Hence the rule of law is only another mask for the rule of a class.[5]

This sociological analysis does not, of course, have to be Marxist in this or any other sense. But the Marxist view does introduce some refinements.

These depend on the notion of the State as an organization created by and serving to protect and promote the interests of the ruling class.[6] Law is the will of that State which seems to stand outside and above society. This seeming independence of the State and therefore of law helps to obscure the real power relationships which are determined by the economic relationships between classes, helps to legitimate the exercise of that power, and enables the State and the law to appear neutral.

Their (the capitalists) personal rule must at the same time be constituted as an average rule. Their personal power is based on conditions of life which as they develop are common to many individuals, and the continuance of which they, as ruling individuals, have to maintain against others and, at the same time, maintain that they hold good for all. The expression of this will, which is determined by their common interests, is law.[7]

For my present purposes, however, this view takes us only some way along the road.

For the function performed by the judiciary in our society is not a peculiarly capitalist function. Some of its manifestations – such as its tenderness towards private property and its dislike of trade unions – may be traced to such a source. But its strong adherence to the maintenance of law and order, its distaste for minority opinions, demonstrations and protests, its indifference to the promotion of better race relations, its support of governmental secrecy, and its concern for the preservation of the moral and social behaviour to which it is accustomed, these attitudes seem to derive from a different ideology.

Moreover if the judicial function in the United Kingdom were wholly capitalist in origin, it would be surprising to find any similarities or even points of comparison with non-capitalist societies. Yet we find the judiciary in non-capitalist societies to be even more a part of their political and economic power groups. The Marxist analysis tells us a great deal about the differences between capitalist and non-capitalist societies but little about the differing roles played by the judges in the two societies. And this is for the excellent reason that the judges perform *similar* functions, reflecting their respective societies.

By this I do not mean that the influence exerted directly on the judiciary by the political arm of the State in the communist countries of Eastern Europe is paralleled by a similar direct influence in the capitalist countries of Western Europe. No doubt, in the great majority of cases before the courts, the judges in communist countries act independently of the Executive and are prepared to invalidate illegal actions by its members. But in the small number of crucial cases where the offences are political the political influence is more obviously direct. And here political offences means offences which may be drawn in broad terms to include conduct deemed detrimental to State interests. Further, I am speaking of the judiciary only and not of the activities of the political police, or of powers to detain without trial. If I were of a radical turn of mind with a leaning towards iconoclasm and a distrust of those in authority, I would (to put it mildly) find more scope and greater continuity for my activities in the capitalist west than in the communist east.

But the relative responsiveness of the judiciary to political pressure is not an attribute or a function specific to capitalism or to communism. It would be easy to name a score of countries which are undeniably capitalist and where the judges are as strongly under the influence of the political Executive as they are in any communist society. That relative responsiveness reflects the extent to which the judges share the aims and values of the political system, and the extent to which they are its enthusiastic supporters.

It is in this sense that I speak of judges in different countries performing similar functions, reflecting their respective societies, and the political power which operates in them.

Again any analysis which places the judiciary in the United Kingdom in a wholly subservient position to the Government misreads history and mistakes the source and nature of the common law. Those who criticize existing institutions in the United Kingdom need always to remember that, in comparison with most other countries, this country enables its citizens to live in comparative freedom. To what extent is this a consequence of our judicial system and of our judges?

That they play some part is undeniable. They will even, on occasion, enforce the law which forbids arrest without reasonable cause or imprisonment without trial, and support the right of free association or, within its limits, of free speech. The idea of the rule of law is not wholly illusory.[8]

There is a sense, however far it falls short of what is claimed for it, in which those who exercise legalized force in our society must have regard to the existence of a judiciary which may be prepared to condemn them in some circumstances and will be supported in so doing. Nevertheless, in the event of an attempt by a Government to exercise arbitrary and extensive powers, curtailing individual liberty, it cannot be forecast how the judges would react. The political circumstances would be crucial and the judiciary would be divided, as Lords Parker and Gardiner were divided over official torture in Northern Ireland (see above, p. 46). A left-wing attempt would meet with judicial opposition more immediately than a right-wing attempt. And there is little evidence to suggest that the judiciary would be quick to spring to the defence of individual liberty wherever the threat came from.

To whatever extent we seek to define more precisely the function of the judiciary in our society so as to take account of the power of judges to act independently of others, their place as part of the governing group remains unaffected. Nor must we lose sight of two major determinants of the whole. The first is that we in the United Kingdom do live in an increasingly authoritarian society and that this quality is the outstanding phenomenon of all modern States. I do not mean to belittle the remarkable achievements in authoritarianism of the great systems of government of the past. But modern authoritarianism deals with millions where the tyrants of the past dealt with thousands. And the means of control today are obviously more scientific and much more thorough. It is within such systems that the judges operate; and they operate to help to run these systems. And authoritarianism is always, by its essential nature, conservative and reactionary. It must preserve itself.

Secondly, judges are the product of a class and have the characteristics of that class. Typically coming from middle-class professional families, independent schools, Oxford or Cambridge, they spend 20 to 25 years in successful practice at the bar, mostly in London, earning very considerable incomes by the time they reach their forties. This is not the stuff of which reformers are made, still less radicals. There are those who believe that if more grammar or comprehensive schoolboys, graduating at redbrick or new glass universities, became barristers and then judges, the judiciary would be that much less conservative. This is extremely doubtful for two reasons.

The years in practice and the middle-aged affluence would remove any aberration in political outlook, if this were necessary. Also, if these changes did not take place, there would be no possibility of their being appointed by the Lord Chancellor, on the advice of the most senior judiciary, to the bench. Ability by itself is not enough. Unorthodoxy in political opinion is a certain disqualification for appointment.

Her Majesty's judges are unlikely to be under great illusions about the functioning of political power in the United Kingdom today. And I think we come close to their definition of the public interest and of the interests of the State if we identify their views with those who insist that in any society, but especially societies in the second half of the twentieth century, stability above all is necessary for the health of the people and is the supreme law.

It follows that Governments are normally to be supported but not in every case. Governments represent stability and have a very considerable interest in preserving it. The maintenance of authoritarian structures in all public institutions is wholly in the interest of Governments. This is true of all Governments of all political complexions, capitalist and communist alike. Whenever Governments or their agencies are acting to preserve that stability – call it the Queen's peace, or law and order, or the rule of law, or whatever – the judges will lend their support and will not be over-concerned if to do so requires the invasion of individual liberty.

When, then, is it justifiable, in the opinion of judges, not to support governmental power? From recent cases, certain generalizations can be drawn. First, none of the decisions which conflict with that power falls within that aspect of the judicial view of the public interest which is concerned to maintain law and order, the pre-eminence of which is wholly preserved. Secondly, the courts seem very willing to intervene when the essence of the plaintiff's case is that he is the victim of an exercise of the political policy of Ministers. Perhaps this is part of that old common law resentment which judges have against statute law. Perhaps it is all that is left of the former tradition of protecting individual liberty. But it is manifested in, for example, the *Laker, Tameside, Padfield, Congreve, Anisminic, Burmah Oil, Lavender,* and *Coleen* decisions (see above, pp. 114-15, 121-9) – so much so that one wonders whether the *Stevenage* decision (see above, p. 112) would have gone the way it did had it been decided within the last ten years.

All those judicial decisions struck down political decisions taken during the period of Labour Governments. It is clearly of some relevance that the first three (and possibly the fourth also) concerned Ministerial decisions which Conservative Ministers might not have taken. But it is doubtful whether the political complexion of the Government had anything to do with the political decisions in the last four. Much more significant is that these eight cases and others reflect the emergence of a period of judicial activism or intervention which began in the early 1960s and has been growing in strength ever since. How far this development has been inspired or assisted by the fact that between 1964 and 1977 Labour Governments have been in office for all but four years is an open question. Perhaps all that can be said is that Labour Governments are more likely than Conservative Governments to act in ways which offend the judicial sense of rightness, the judicial view of where the public interest lies.

It is interesting to speculate how far the judges would be willing to push their opposition to the Government of the day if convinced that its policies were contrary to the public interest, and how far the Government would permit such opposition to continue. Lord Devlin, writing about the *Padfield* decision, wondered 'whether the courts have moved too far from their base' which, he said, was 'the correction of abuse'. He continued, and here he was also speaking of the *Tameside* decision:

One may also share to some extent the apprehensions of the Civil Service. All legal history shows that, once the judges get a foothold in the domain of fact, they move to expand. Questions of fact become in a mysterious way questions of law. The fence between error and misconception crumbles with the passage of time. The civil servant may fear the day when he dare not reach a conclusion without asking himself whether a judge will think all the deciding factors as relevant as he does. I do not think that the judiciary should be thrust out of the domain of fact.

Lord Devlin wanted above all to see judicial review 'preserved as a weapon against arbitrary government and I am conscious that its efficacy depends upon the good will of Whitehall'. Because of the power of Government to exclude judicial review by statutory provision 'judicial interference with the executive cannot for long very greatly exceed what Whitehall will accept'.[9]

The ultimate, if partial, subservience of the judiciary to the Government is spelt out clearly in those words. But the phraseology seems to me greatly to overstate, by implication, the willingness or the desire of judges to control 'arbitrary' government. Behind the administrative difficulties which the Minister foresaw in *Tameside*, and the consequent harm to groups of pupils, lay the principle of comprehensive schooling. There, as in the cases arising out of legislation concerned with housing and planning, trade unions, and race relations, the judiciary digs its trenches against what it sees as government not in the public interest. But *Padfield*, *Tameside* and *Laker*, though significant of the modern trend towards greater judicial intervention, are still untypical. They represent the judicial desire not so much to control arbitrariness as to protect the individual against political policies which are seen by the judiciary to be contrary to the public interest.

Lord Justice Scarman's plea for the introduction of a Bill of Rights is relevant here.[10] The purposes he has in mind may be wholly admirable being based largely on the Universal Declaration of Human Rights. But others who have also spoken in favour of such a Bill, whose provisions would be entrenched and only repealable or declared inapplicable with the approval of a special (perhaps two-thirds) majority in Parliament, have amongst other things hoped it would prevent the curtailment of freedom of speech in the Race Relations Acts, the educational policies of the Labour Government which denied parental choice, the rights of entry of factory and health inspectors, and a tax policy, the effect of which would be (it was claimed) to destroy a substantial proportion of independent businesses.[11]

The European Convention of Human Rights, also a candidate for entrenchment in our law, after listing a number of desirable purposes adds provisos to each in terms like:

No restrictions shall be placed on the exercise of these rights other than such as are prescribed by law and are necessary in a democratic society in the interests of national security or public safety, for the prevention of disorder or crime, for the protection of health or morals or for the protection of the rights and freedom of others. This Article shall not prevent the imposition of lawful restrictions on the exercise of these rights by members of the armed forces, of the police or of the administration of the State.

It is difficult to see how the welfare of the individual would be promoted by the enactment of such provisions if they were to be interpreted by the judiciary of today.

Nevertheless, the approach to an examination of the nature of judicial power through a consideration of human rights had, for the British political system in the mid-1970s, an air of novelty. Liberal thinking among the judiciary has, as we have seen, shown itself only occasionally and then only in minority judgments or dissents. The protection of the public interest in the preservation of a stable society is how the judges see their role.

In other eyes their view of the public interest appears merely as reactionary conservatism. It is not the politics of the extreme right. Its insensitivity is clearly rooted more in unconscious assumptions than in a wish to oppress. But it is demonstrable that on every major social issue which has come before the courts during the last 30 years – concerning industrial relations, political protest, race relations, government secrecy, police powers, moral behaviour – the judges have supported the conventional, established, and settled interests. And they have reacted strongly against challenges to those interests. This conservatism does not necessarily follow the day-to-day political policies currently associated with the party of that name. But it is a political philosophy nonetheless.

My thesis, then, is that the judiciary in any modern industrial society, however composed, under whatever economic system, is an essential part of the system of government and that its function may be described as underpinning the stability of that system and as protecting that system from attack by resisting attempts to change it.

Many regard the values of the bench and bar as wholly admirable and the spirit of the common law (as presently expressed) to be a national adornment. The incorruptibility of the English bench and its independence of the Government are great virtues. All this is not in issue. When I argue that they regard the interests of the State or the public interest as pre-eminent and that they interpret those interests as meaning that, with very few exceptions, established authority must be upheld and that those exceptions are made only when a more conservative position can be adopted, this does not mean that the judges are acting with impropriety. It means that we live in a highly authoritarian society, fortunate only that we do not live in other societies which are even more authoritarian. We must expect judges, as part of that authority, to act in the interests, as they see them, of the social order.

The judges define the public interest, inevitably, from the viewpoint of their own class. And those interests, by a natural, not an artificial, coincidence, are the interests of others in authority, whether in Government, in the City or in the Church. Those values are the maintenance of law and order, the protection of private property, the containment of the trade union movement, and the continuance of Governments which conduct their business largely in private and on the advice of other members of what I have called the governing group.

Far more than on the judiciary, our freedoms depend on the willingness of the press, politicians and others to publicize the breach of these freedoms and on the continuing vulnerability of Ministers, civil servants, the police, other public officials and powerful private interests to accusations that these freedoms are being infringed. In other words, we depend far more on the political climate and on the vigilance of those members of society who for a variety of reasons, some political and some humanitarian, make it their business to seek to hold public authorities within their proper limits. That those limits are also prescribed by law and that judges may be asked to maintain them is not without significance. But the judges are not, as in a different dispensation and under a different social order they might be, the strong, natural defenders of liberty.

Judges are concerned to preserve and to protect the existing order. This does not mean that no judges are capable of moving with the times, of adjusting to changed circumstances. But their function in our society is to do so belatedly. Law and order, the established distribution of power both public and private, the conventional and agreed view amongst those who exercise political and economic power, the fears and prejudices of the middle and upper classes, these are the forces which the judges are expected to uphold and do uphold.

I am not sure what would be the attitude of judges in the ideal society. Perhaps they would not be needed because conflict between Government and the governed would have been removed. But in the societies of our world today they do not stand out as protectors of liberty, of the rights of man, of the unprivileged. With very few notable exceptions, judges in South Africa or Rhodesia, in India, in the Soviet Union, in western Europe, in Chile, and elsewhere have not shown that they are 'no respecters of persons and stand between the subject and any attempted encroachments on his liberty by the executive'[12]; nor have they insisted that holders of great economic power, private or public, should use it with moderation. Their view of the public interest, when it has gone beyond the interest of Governments, has not been wide enough to embrace the interests of political, ethnic, social or other minorities. Only occasionally, in the United States of America, has the power of the supreme judiciary been exercised in the positive assertion of fundamental values. In both capitalist and communist societies, the judiciary has naturally served the prevailing political and economic forces. Politically, judges are parasitic.

That this is so is not a matter for recrimination. It is idle to criticize institutions for performing the task they were created to perform and have performed for centuries. It is possible to criticize the police if they use excessive force or illegal means in maintaining law and order, but to criticize them for fulfilling their function is absurd. So also with the judiciary. Their principal function is to support the institutions of government as established by law. To expect a judge to advocate radical change, albeit legally, is as absurd as it would be to expect an anarchist to speak up in favour of an authoritarian society. The confusion arises when it is pretended that judges are somehow neutral in the conflicts between those who challenge existing institutions and those who control those institutions. And cynicism replaces confusion whenever it becomes apparent that the latter are using the judges as open allies in those conflicts.

Thus it is usual for judges in political cases to be able

to rely on the rules of law for the legitimacy of their decisions. As we have seen, there are innumerable ways – through the development of the common law, the interpretation of statutes, the refusal to use discretionary powers, the claims to residual jurisdiction and the rest – in which the judges can fulfil their political function and do so in the name of the law.

NOTES

1. As in the foregoing parts of this book, I am speaking in this part primarily of judges of the High Court, the Court of Appeal and the House of Lords.

2. The *Sunday Times* 6 August 1972.

3. *Prohibitions del Roy* (1607) 12 Co. Rep. 63.

4. See *The Times* 3 July 1976; and the *Guardian* 5 July 1976.

5. E. P. Thompson, *Whigs and Hunters* (1975), p. 259.

6. For a useful summary see Maureen Cain, 'The Main Themes of Marx's and Engels's Sociology of Law' in 1 *British Journal of Law & Society* 136 to which I am indebted.

7. Marx and Engels, *The German Ideology* (1965 edn.) p. 358 quoted by M. Cain *op. cit.*

8. Cf. E. P. Thompson, *op. cit.*, pp. 258-69.

9. *The Times* 27 October 1976.

10. Sir Leslie Scarman, *English Law, the new dimension.*

11. See the examples collected in M. Zander, *A Bill of Rights?*

12. Lord Atkin in *Liversidge v. Anderson* (see above p. 79).

Index

Index

Index

Cases

Cases